When we were jungle training, preparing for our deployment into Southeast Asia in 1965, we all discovered that those who could maintain a sense of humor did better through all the tough stuff. In light of that I have never met a chaplain who served in 'Nam that didn't have a keen sense of humor, and it took me many years to realize the kind of "tough stuff" these dedicated men went through—for us. Larry Haworth is no exception. His writing has the glow of a man dedicated to serving with a smile through the tough stuff, and gritting his teeth even when the red dust has turned to mud in his mouth. This is a book that everyone can enjoy and learn from. I look forward to more of his wonderful ministry in future writings.

Chuck Dean, Vietnam vet
Author, *Nam Vet: Making Peace with Your Past*

Tales of Thunder Run is a collection of short stories familiar to all veterans and also easily understood by non veterans alike. Starting with an example any vet can relate to, Chaplain Haworth relates wartime experiences, causing the reader to examine his own past and wartime experience, and then gently and firmly points out a biblical truth from the story. This book is much more than a daily devotional. It causes the reader to reflect on the past and offers a refreshing perspective.

Dana Morgan, Vietnam vet
President, Point Man International Ministries

D1300722

TALES OF
†HUNDER
RUN

TALES OF THUNDER RUN

The convoys, the noise,
the ambushes...
stories of QL 13, the Route 66 of Viet Nam

LARRY HAWORTH, CHAPLAIN (RET.) USA

ACW Press
Eugene, Oregon 97405

Tales of Thunder Run
Copyright ©2004 Lawrence E. Haworth, Chaplain (ret), USA
All rights reserved

Cover Design by Alpha Advertising
Interior Design by Pine Hill Graphics

Packaged by ACW Press
85334 Lorane Hwy
Eugene, Oregon 97405
www.acwpress.com
The views expressed or implied in this work do not necessarily reflect those of ACW Press. Ultimate design, content, and editorial accuracy of this work is the responsibility of the author(s).

Library of Congress Cataloging-in-Publication Data
(Provided by Cassidy Cataloguing Services, Inc.)

Haworth, Larry.

   Tales of Thunder Run : the convoys, the noise, the ambushes : stories of QL 13, the Route 66 of Viet Nam / Larry Haworth. -- 1st ed. -- Eugene, Ore. : ACW Press, 2004.

   p. ; cm.

   ISBN: 1-932124-24-1

   1. Vietnamese Conflict, 1961-1975--Personal narratives.
2. Vietnamese Conflict, 1961-1975--Chaplains--Biography. 3. United States. Army--History--Vietnamese Conflict, 1961-1975. 4. Vietnam--History--1945-1975. 5. United States. Army--Chaplains--Biography.
I. Title.

DS559.5 .H39 2004
959.704/3373--dc22   0401

Printed in the United States of America.

dedication

This book is dedicated to every young man and woman who answered their country's call, wore the uniform, and served with honor. Some went into harm's way and others served in peace. Some gave more than others, but all did what their country asked. What more could they do?

contents

preface

IN 1969 I RETURNED TO VIET NAM FOR MY SECOND TOUR of duty in that beautiful, war-torn land. I had served a first tour in the Mekong Delta with combat aviation at Soc Trang during the period of the Tet Offensive of '68. From there I was assigned, at my request, to Fort Ord, California, where I served as chaplain for Infantry Advanced Individual Training with a great chaplain, Roy Peters. He had requested a second tour to Viet Nam which I thought was a good idea. He was a lieutenant colonel and I was only a captain. My request was honored with orders within *five days,* which must have been a record for the Chief's office. Roy went later. I requested an infantry unit in Viet Nam, what with ministering with infantry trainees and all. They put me in the cav instead, armored cavalry. What did I know? I thought cavalry was John Wayne, the Lone Ranger and the Old West. I soon found out what armored cav was really all about, at least in the jungles of Viet Nam and Cambodia while riding with the Blackhorse. And what a great and wild ride that was! I quickly became convinced that ours was the best squadron or battalion in the whole U.S. Army during the leadership of LTC Grail Brookshire and MAJ Fred Franks. I still believe it. Much of our mission was centered along QL 13, a major highway leading from Saigon into Cambodia. Chapter one will tell you about it. We called it Thunder Run, hence the name of this book as well as the quarterly newsletter put out by the 11th Armored Cavalry Veterans of Viet Nam and Cambodia. I've been honored to be their chaplain since our first reunion in Dallas in 1986.

This book is written with more than cavalry vets in mind. Each chapter is based on vignettes from the jungles and rice paddies of Viet Nam under combat conditions. These vignettes are memories and stories that I hope all vets everywhere can relate to with pleasure and good memories. Because they are real and of a positive nature and they reflect life as we experienced it, my intention is that families and others interested in that lifestyle will gain a little understanding of what life was like in that place and in those days. I hope vets of other wars and eras will relate too. Maybe these vignettes and anecdotes will help them remember and tell their stories too with pride and sometimes even a little humor.

Of course, being a chaplain and a committed Christian, I always add a spiritual cap with a verse or two from the Holy Bible to finish off each chapter. I'm very aware that many vets (and others) don't like to have religion pushed in their face. I try hard to not be "in your face." I also try to be forthright and honest. Vets prefer their information "on top of the table," clear, honest, and to the point. I try to be that way. Many felt very acutely that they were messed with. Some were. So I try to avoid messing with anyone. But I do want to get my point in. Check it for yourself. One of my purposes for having been born is to introduce others to the person of Jesus Christ. I try to do this in such a way that he is real for them, but not in an obnoxious way. For those who want nothing to do with the religious part, that's OK. I hope you enjoy what I have to say too. I was there for everyone. Like one of my vets said a couple of years ago, "Chaplain, I never went to any of your services out there in the jungle. But I appreciated that you came. That way I had a choice." Well put, trooper. I was there for you too.

God bless you. God loves you. So do I.

Chaplain Larry Haworth

foreword

HERE IS A STOREHOUSE OF THE TALES THAT MADE THE men of the Blackhorse regiment famous, even from afar and now a generation of soldiers ago. Battle and boredom in unequal proportions, with all the privations, esprit de corps, suffering, death, triumph, and quiet anonymity except among those who were there and knew the deal.

Those of us then in training or preparing for Vietnam grew up in the army on these tales—our daily bread and standard fare, upon which we listened or read in countless hours to learn of their courage and tactical acumen—what we hoped to be or to become or to emulate when it came our time for 'Nam: what worked and what didn't. And we all knew that our own time was coming, such was the army in those days: you were either going, coming back, or getting ready to go. Nonetheless, many of us did not go to Vietnam, but came to wear the famous Blackhorse patch elsewhere in other times—in Germany, in Kuwait, in the Mojave at Fort Irwin, and even in Afghanistan in another dirty, but no less dangerous war. The fact that so many did not fight in the jungles of south east Asia casts a dim generational curtain that raises these tales of combat to a status apart , where the legend and the fact became one. "Father Larry" AKA "Saint Six" raises that curtain and illuminates the story of these Blackhorse troopers through the chaplain's all seeing eyes with a wit and casual charm that bespeaks the élan of the cavalry troopers with whom he served and with whom he still serves today as the chaplain for the Blackhorse troopers who served in Vietnam. Moreover, these stories have the uplifting value of the true heart and spirit of the American fighting man: love of country, love of one another, and love of God—where all were put to the stern test of battle. A great read, a wonderful legacy of service to God and country under fire.

Julian "JB" Burns
Major General, USA

thunder run

OLD US HIGHWAY 66. DOES THAT SAY ANYTHING TO you? It sure does to me. Many call it America's highway (or something like that). It cuts across the heartland of America from Los Angeles to Chicago through the Midwestern bread-basket farm states. When I was a kid we travelled it from L.A. to Oklahoma to see my dad's family out on the farm where he was raised. My dad was a dust bowl Okie who rode the rails and migrated along 66 to California during the Depression. I suppose some of you have travelled it too. Hollywood even produced the old black and white TV series, *Hiway 66*, about two young guys in a Corvette who had great adventures along that old highway before the interstates replaced it.

US Highway 66 reminds me of Viet Nam Highway QL 13. Know what I mean? A lot happened along US 66 in those days that I'll always remember. Same with QL 13 in Viet Nam. Some would say the same about Highway 1 that went through Xuan Loc to Da Nang and points north. I was never on it myself, except for one quick trip to Blackhorse Base Camp when I came into country. I went up to Quan Loi right away and never came back. Anyway, a lot of Blackhorse history took place along QL 13. We even named our newspaper "Thunder Run" in honor of the name we dubbed QL13. I guess the Blackhorse armored cavalry passing through was like thunder in a monsoon. Right? The convoys, the noise, the ambushes, the dust (eating dirt—remember?), the mud, the outposts, the mama-sans, the Lambrettas and red Honda 50s, the villages, the fields of fire (clearings made that way by Agent Orange), the rubber trees, the mines, the bridges, the arc lights in the distance, the twisted French railroad tracks that ran beside the highway. I guess Thunder Run had been a beautiful highway before the war and Agent Orange. It's probably beautiful again now.

I think QL13 started somewhere down around Saigon. I know we convoyed once from Loc Ninh to Di An and took QL13 through Lai Khe to get there. Anyway, let's talk about those French railroad tracks I mentioned. Remember how twisted and pathetic they looked? They were torn apart and lying alongside QL13 like the ghost of a former age, a lost war, an old culture that would never come back. Whether that was good or bad, who knows? Still, I used to look at those old tracks and wonder about life along that antique railroad in its heyday. I imagined those French narrow-gauge trains running and carrying people and stuff all over Southeast Asia. Some people think we ended up like the French, leaving with our tails between our legs. I don't buy that myself. I believe the place is a lot better now than it would have been if we hadn't come along. That's saying a lot because so much craziness happened over there. Still does, only not as bad as it was right after we left. Check the people these days. Check how they love American GIs, even now. Take a trip over there and you'll see. Check how they love jeans and American tourists. Check how they love American music. Check how they love American ideals like wanting freedom to come into the twenty-first century. Check how they want to learn computers and English, American English. We didn't count for anything? We didn't make the place better? Sure we did. (I'll stop this now because I'm getting in deeper than I want.)

Some of you were along one day when our combat engineers were minesweeping QL 13 down from Loc Ninh and up from Quan Loi. Our minesweepers were slow because they were on foot, of course. QL 13 was a busy highway and the work slowed traffic considerably. Then we had to stop to repair a culvert across the road which the VC had blown the night before. We brought up an AVLB to lay across the culvert so traffic could go by while our engineers laid a new culvert. Trouble came when the Vietnamese backed up behind our guys got impatient. They decided they couldn't wait for us to clear the road of mines. I don't remember every detail, but I do remember that seven of those colorful Vietnamese buses passed us by in a mighty hurry. They just couldn't wait for the road to be cleared. You guessed it. We looked up after a few minutes. About a mile ahead we could see an explosion. We knew somebody had hit a mine. We couldn't get up there to help them very fast because we still had to clear the road. Before we got to the explosion site, we found three more mines in the road. The third bus in line had hit the fourth mine in the road. The other buses and traffic were fortunate. They all should have been blown to smithereens. But they weren't. Only one bus got it. The other buses, trucks, and Lambrettas got off clean. The mined bus had casualties all over the place which I don't need to describe. Pretty soon families got the word and came down from Loc Ninh. Not a fun time.

There are plenty of fine memories of QL13, of course. Yes, there are many good memories from Viet Nam. Like the day we came out of Cambodia. Were you there? We'd been in Cambodia for exactly two months. President Nixon had finally allowed our side to go into that Communist sanctuary. He gave us two months to do what we could to take it out. Our guys did a lot considering that it was years late and we only had two months. I admit our troopers didn't take it out 100 percent like we wanted, but our side sure did slow down the Communist side. We could have cleaned up the whole mess, but our political side decided to "negotiate" instead. But never mind that. QL 13 was still our way out of Cambodia. Not the way in. The Fish Hook was the way in. Coming *out* was a lot easier than going *in* had been. It was a pretty cheerful day, as I recall. We came out of Cambodia and just kept on moving. We went on past Loc Ninh, past Quan Loi, past Lai Khe and past a lot of old ambush and firefight sites too. Funny thing, we went on past engineers that were actually paving over QL13. Guess it wouldn't be Thunder Run any more. At least there wouldn't be so much thunder. Our days in the AO were over. We were going down to beat the bush around Long Binh and then start phasing out of country altogether. Took a couple more years, but it happened.

So, a lot happened along QL13, *Thunder Run*. Hundreds of stories could be told by you troopers who made the run. Like the E Troop ambush near QL13 south of Quan Loi in August of '69 when John Sexton was taken POW—and kept locked up for two and a half years in remote jungle camps in Cambodia. Or like branching off QL13 at Loc Ninh to go up QL14 to Bo Duc and Bu Dop to clear that overgrown highway so the Vietnamese could use it again. Stories about that too. Or like convoying along QL13 to go on a rare stand-down, a once-a-year, if ever, happening to get the machinery operating right again. Remember? I guess if most of the reminiscences at reunions were just about what happened along Thunder Run, it would fill a year of talking and remembering. And for you troopers who didn't do QL13, you did Hiway 1 or Another Run. Those were wild rides too.

One thing about Thunder Run. It was always a wild ride. You didn't always know how it was going to wind up, especially when you ran into an ambush or had a few RPGs aimed your way. But you sure knew where you were going when you were on that run. Off the road you could lose your way. I saw it happen. But when that track, that ACav, M48, M548, Hog, or Sheridan was running down the center of QL13, whichever direction didn't matter, you knew exactly where you were headed. It was a ride you'll remember for a lifetime.

Life itself is sort of like Thunder Run, QL13. Many memories, many adventures, many experiences, many relationships. It's like riding with the Blackhorse along that run—you can see where you're going. Just stay on the road, fix your eyes straight ahead and keep on truckin' (or tankin'). And when it gets to where the rubber really hits the road of life, the wise trooper will examine his direction, check his map and see where he is on his Life's Run or whether he's off the course for where he wants to go. When we consider that every one of us is on the road of life and we're heading somewhere, it's wise and reasonable to check the destination of the road you're on. If you know me, you'll know I recommend taking the road that leads to life, to God. Eternal life with God your Creator. A quote from Jesus the Messiah, the Son of God makes the life map clear: "Don't be troubled. You trust God, now trust in me. There are many rooms in my Father's home, and I am going to prepare a place for you. If this were not so, I would tell you plainly. When everything is ready, I will come and get you, so that you will always be with me where I am. And you know where I am going and how to get there. 'No we don't know, Lord,' Thomas said. 'We haven't any idea where you are going, so how can we know the way?' Jesus told him, 'I am the way, the truth, and the life. No one can come to the Father except through me.'" (John 14:1-6 NIV).

Well, QL13, Thunder Run, is full of meaning and memories, whatever our experiences, whatever our adventures along that road. They stick with us to this day. Our lives were changed for all time. We grew up. We learned life. We learned what life meant in very many ways. I trust and pray that, whatever your experiences along Thunder Run, you are better for it. I also trust and pray for each of you, in a similar way, that all of your life has its fullest meaning. That meaning is in its greatest adventure, which is with God our Creator keeping us in the center of the way, right on course until the very end.

2

a matter of perspective

My first tour in Viet Nam was in 1967-68. I was assigned to the 13th Combat Aviation Battalion at Soc Trang in the Mekong Delta. There were more than six hundred chaplains in country at the time. I was the southernmost of them all except for one who visited a MACV team at Bac Lieu or some that occasionally went out with American troops in the U Minh Forest. People talked about Saigon as being down south. Can Tho was "way down in the Delta." To us, Saigon was eighty air miles north. Can Tho was thirty-five air miles north. We always talked about air miles because you couldn't drive the roads, except for convoys, because of the mines. I liked Soc Trang just fine. I was chaplain to a great bunch of soldiers and a few dedicated donut dollies. We supported ARVN infantry. The closest American ground units were based way north at My Tho. Soc Trang was where I did Tet '68, a great party that many of you were "invited" to and had the memorable thrill of attending. My opinion was that Soc Trang was a great place to be, if you were going to be in Viet Nam. Troops serving up north thought we were at one of the far ends of the earth. We were. My supervisory chaplain came down from Saigon to help me out one time. His plane got shot at and took a round through the tail. He never came back! How you look at a place and how you feel about it in your gut is a matter of your personal experience and perspective. That also determines how it affected you then and how it affects you now.

My second tour was with the Blackhorse. It was a lot different. That was 1969-70. We got to go into Cambodia that time. We really made some memories. I guess that's what they call "the good old days." Anyway, riding around the jungle on the bustle rack of an M-48 or on the driver's hatch lid (cover) of an ACav sure gave me a different perspective from flying around in a Huey in the gunner's well or riding along in the back seat of a Bird Dog spotter plane. I don't mind telling you, I never did figure which of those gave me the tightest pucker factor when the shooting started. In the air there's nowhere to hide. You know the tracers are all aimed at you because no one else is around. On top of that, for every tracer you see, you remember there are four you don't see. And all of them are for you. On the other hand, one time I was on the ground minding my own business going to the bathroom on the berm at four in the morning. Someone decided to shoot at me with an RPG. That was pretty high on the pucker scale too! The perspective may be different, but it still gives you something to tell your grandkids about.

Other people have different experiences. Some memorable. Some traumatic. Some mundane. Some life changing. Some we forget five minutes after the fact. Some we talk about and get it rinsed out of our system. Some we stuff and pay for later. We said, "It don't mean nuthin," when it really meant plenty. Then we get on with our life with new perspectives we didn't have before.

We come home. Someone says, "Welcome Home." Or no one says, "Welcome Home." We go back to school. We get a job. We get married. We get divorced. We stay married. We have kids. We don't have kids. We get a dog. We go fishing. We go into the woods. We don't go into the woods. We pick up where we left off—NOT. Whatever else happens as we get on with our lives, we are different. We don't just pick up where we left off. We have gained a new and far different perspective on what life is all about. We are not the same. We can never be the same. We don't need to be the same. We don't want to be the same. Because we have seen life from a perspective the protected will never know. Before we went we were one of the protected. Not now. Not ever again.

What you do about this changed perspective on life will determine how you live the rest of your life. It will determine the quality of your life—and of your family and everyone around you that you love and who love you. We all know a lot more about what's important in life than we ever could have known before we went through the fire. Trouble is, some of us get hung up on the traumas and the negatives of life. We live, over and over again, the tough times—the real tough times. Some keep living there and can't seem to move on. They don't put matters in perspective with the rest of their life. This sort of trooper needs to accept the help, healing, forgiveness, and support that are out there so he can put life in perspective and get on with it. It can be done. Many are doing it. There *are* answers. Keep reading. Keep looking.

We all can use our experiences and the perspectives we gained, including the big ones, to make life better for others along with ourselves. God doesn't allow us to go through hell for absolutely no reason at all. We talk about this in other places too (see "Where was God?" in chapter 28). When we see all of life in perspective and put each time, experience, situation, and relationship in its proper place, we can see what life's all about and find satisfaction and peace of mind. Viet Nam will always be an extremely important part of our lives. For most, I think it will be a defining time. It was for me. I've had many life-changing experiences before and since but, aside from accepting Jesus Christ as my personal Savior, my Viet Nam experience defined a lot of what my purpose in life was all about. It still does. At the same time, I get on with life because, important as it is, Viet Nam is not my *whole* life. Nor should it be yours.

Finally, I will point out that no one's life can be complete and reach its ultimate purpose apart from the spiritual part. And I don't mean just feeling good or doing nice things. I mean including Almighty God in the very fabric of who you are. Only God gives ultimate meaning. Only God gave you life and existence. Only God sees all of creation from an eternal perspective. That's where we get our highest perspective on life, including our Viet Nam experience. Many answers I don't have, but the God part I know. I accept the big answers about life on the authority of the Bible. That got me through tight times in Viet Nam. Tight times since then, too (also the easy times).

Anyway, I sincerely hope each of us will take a look at our lives from an honest and mature perspective. We are at an age now where we have some years and a track record behind us. Ahead of us too. This helps a whole lot in seeing life for how it really is. We're not young and green anymore. We've come a long way. Most of us have a long way left to go. Life is better when we keep things in perspective and when we remember we are not alone. In the words of the Savior, "Surely, I am with you always, to the end of the age."

Think about it. OK?

3

counting time

WHERE DID YOU GO TO GRAMMAR SCHOOL? I WENT TO Tarzana Elementary School in, you guessed it, Tarzana. It's part of Los Angeles in Southern California. That was in the days before the Fruits and Nuts moved to California. Except that I'm probably one of the Nuts. But I'm not one of the Fruits—they came later. Anyway, those were memorable years. When I was a little kid the high school kids were sure *big*. I remember riding with my folks past Canoga Park High School and thinking, "I'll never get big enough to go to that scary place." Next thing you know, there I was, *graduating* from that same high school. I don't know where the time went, but it sure went! Now here I sit, half a century later, trying to figure what happened to the time. That's my youthful story. What's yours? It's probably similar to mine.

Time sure takes on a different perspective when you grow older and get into different situations. Remember the Viet Nam War years? (Like, who could forget?) Maybe you were drafted. Maybe you volunteered for whatever reason. Maybe the judge told you to join the Army or go to jail (Huh?) Maybe you were a lifer. Maybe you put in for the Blackhorse 11th Armored Cavalry Regiment. Maybe you didn't. Maybe you never heard of the Blackhorse before you got there. Maybe the only black horse you ever heard of was Black Beauty. Maybe you're not old enough to know about Black Beauty. Maybe all you knew of the cavalry was what you saw in John Wayne movies. Maybe this and maybe that. But I bet you remember your trip going over there. Going to the Nam, I mean. I sure remember, especially the first time. I was nervous, naturally. I flew. (In an airplane. What did you think?) I wasn't a boat person. When we got into Vietnamese air space, I looked down and got scared almost spitless. Well, a little dry-mouthed, anyway. I saw those bomb craters all over the place and I thought we were going to get shot out of the sky for sure, which we didn't. We made the normal quick descent because our TWA airliner crew thought they were in the war. Which, in a way, they were. (We had TWA's senior stewardess on board—she liked us.) Anyway, we got off the plane fast, they loaded up again and took off real soon. At least, I think they did. I was too busy being nervous to really notice.

Here's the main thing I was nervous about besides maybe getting shot at: I kept thinking how can I get through a whole year of this? Is that what you thought too? Well, my second tour was with the Blackhorse. (First tour was with helicopters and Bird Dog spotter planes in the Delta.) Second tour and first tour were the same question: "How can I make it through a whole year of this?" Know what? I did make it. So did you. One way or the other, we made it. Some didn't, of course. I'm humbled to remember with respect and honor the troopers that didn't make it. We honor them every year with a memorial service. We honor their families too. We also honor and remember our POWs and MIAs. We will *never* forget them.

Meanwhile, we proceed with our lives. These fast moving lives we live. A few weeks ago I saw a cartoon of a middle-aged (or old-aged) man looking in a mirror. He was saying, "But I wasn't finished being young yet!" That could be me. You're probably saying the same thing. "But I'm not through being young yet!" Could be you. Time keeps marching on no matter what.

Does it seem like thirty or thirty-five-plus years since you were in Viet Nam? Maybe it does sometimes. But I bet most often it doesn't seem that long ago to you. It sure doesn't to me. Sometimes I get to thinking about life between then and now. Marriage, kids, jobs, promotions, moving, losing jobs, having problems with memories, maybe even PTSD, self medicating, getting divorced, getting sick, getting well, retiring, taking vacations and so on and so forth. What about thinking about God? Where does God fit in? What about thinking about Jesus Christ and life's meaning? What about thinking about life's blessings? What about thinking about how you show love to your grandkids? What about retiring and going fishing? What about healing relationships that've been fractured for years? What about making sure your kids know for sure that you love them? What about making for double sure that your spouse, namely your wife, knows for sure that you love her? (The other way around if you're a woman reading this.) All these things matter. They add up to a life. Your life. My life.

We're at the stage now where we can look back and see life in a perspective we never had before. We're not young bucks any more. We may like to come to reunions and think we're the same as in the old days. But we're not. It's not just your old buddy who's lost his hair and grown a pouch (or paunch). Check the mirror, side profile. Time hasn't passed you by, either. It's carried you along. Me too. We're all in this together, this life of passing time. There's one inescapable truth about life, your life, my life, everybody's life. It's measured in units of time. Segments of time. Minutes, hours, days, weeks, years. Time is the same for everybody. And at the end of every trail, time ends for everybody. That's where eternity begins. For everybody. So I guess a point of all this is to make the most of the time we've got. Which is measured the same way for everybody, like I said. Maybe our wealth isn't the same as the next guy, but our stockpile of time is sure the same. That is, until the end. There's no guarantee where the end of your trail is. Just that it is there. It will come.

Back to my first tour in Viet Nam. When I was at the beginning of it I wasn't sure the year would ever go by. But it did. Then after ten months at Fort Ord I was back in Viet Nam again. This time I was with the Blackhorse living in a tent with the 2/11th ACR out in the jungles along the Cambodian border. I thought that tour would never end, either. Especially when we were getting shot at or some other such interesting activity was occurring. But both of those tours did end. Then I went to Germany with the 14th which became the 11th ACR. I thought those tours would never end either. But they did. They were great tours. Hard, but great. And they ended. I thought twenty years in the Army would never end. But it did, and more. I did twenty-seven years (plus four months and three days). That ended too.

I hope and pray to God that those Army years were productive years and pleasing in God's sight. I hope I fulfilled my purpose for living. Then I went back to work again and went back into retirement again too. This time for good, I guess. I hope my working years as a civilian were productive too. Wasn't all work. Some play. Some relaxation. Much enjoyment. But productive and constructive too. You see, I'm one who believes that every man and woman born on this earth has a purpose. That includes you and me. I hope and pray that I've met my purpose. Clearly, since God created us, God gives us our purpose. I hope and pray that I've lived my created purpose. I hope and pray the same for you.

Viet Nam thirty-five years (plus) ago is done and over. Likewise, our lives between then and now are done and over. Our lives here and now will soon enough be done and over too. That's not fatalistic, it's realistic. What I'm wanting is to make the most of it, to get the most out of it, to contribute the most I can while life lasts. I want to enjoy life and, mainly, I do. Then, when I get to the end of my trail, I truly hope to hear the words from God to me, "Well done, good and faithful servant!... Come and share your master's happiness!" (Matthew 26:23). I hope you want that too.

I'll finish off by giving you a few verses from the Old Testament of the Holy Bible. I think you'll agree that these verses are significant, even in the twenty-first century (like, where did the twentieth century go?) You can check these verses out in the very interesting Bible book of Ecclesiastes, which was written by King Solomon: "There is a time for everything, and a season for every activity under heaven.... Whatever is has already been, and what will be has been before; and God will call the past to account.... Now all has been heard; here is the conclusion of the matter: Fear God and keep his commandments, for this is the whole duty of man. For God will bring every deed into judgment, including every hidden thing, whether it is good or evil" (From Ecclesiastes 3:1, 15; 12:13-14 NIV).

margaret

STRANGE, ISN'T IT, THE THINGS YOU SOMETIMES REMEM-
ber from Viet Nam when you get to thinking about it. I know
we repress a lot, forget a lot, and see much of the whole thing
as negative or even traumatic. But a great deal of the experience was positive; even enjoyable or fun and easy to think
about. Remember the rubber flies? No, they weren't made of
rubber. If you were there, you know. They were flies that were
short, fat, and lived in the rubber tree plantations. When we
were operating there during the dry season these rubber flies
would swarm all over us because we were sweating so much
and the flies loved it. They stung and were extremely pesky
critters. But we'd just laugh, swat them and call them names.
Bad names, of course. No problem. Funny to look back on.

One of my pleasant memories is of Margaret. She was
the cutest little thing. Small and petite. She had dark eyes and
such an appealing face. One look and you'd absolutely melt.
And that body. Such a body. Made you just want to hold her
and hug her. Which many of the guys did. Especially out in
the jungle when things got really lonely and quiet. She rode
with a young soldier exclusively on his track, although many
of the guys shared her affections. But there were more of
them than of her and her kind. I remember clearly what she
looked like. I well remember her personality too—so warm

and caring. I also remember when she changed. That was when she became pregnant. The day she had the puppies she seemed to go from being a lovable little puppy to an adult, serious-minded mother dog. She was still as lovable and friendly. But with her new family responsibilities, her soldier left her in base camp and found another pet to take to the field.

Yes, Margaret was a dog. What a great little animal! Many of the soldiers had pets. Pets were a great way for a GI to find comfort and express affection when he was away from the familiarities and comforts of home and friends. Guys had dogs, snakes, monkeys or most anything they could tame— not cats, of course, which couldn't be tamed. One trooper even had a chicken he'd found in Cambodia. It had been left behind by the NVA/VC. It was the ugliest, scrawniest chicken I'd ever seen that wasn't dead beside the road. It had red skin and was missing half its feathers. But "Charlie Chicken" was loved and adopted by G Troop and found a place in many hearts.

Whether you were there or somewhere else, you can understand full well that everyone needs a sense of love and emotional well-being. In a combat environment with all men, and a situation of danger and constant alert, emotional expression is basic. These pets provided for a large degree of that need. It was a pleasure to watch and enjoy. Even at home we have our horses, dogs, cats, birds, and even fish that help fill that emotional need for expressing affection and love.

A psychologist I once knew put it well. He said every person has a basic need to give and receive love. This certainly goes along well with the Bible's teaching that God is love and that humankind is made in the image of God. This means that we all need love because it is how we are made. Even soldiers on the battlefield. Even their families on the home front.

In Viet Nam as with every other war, we know time and time again of instances of incredible acts of bravery or selflessness based on one man or woman's love for their fellow man. There were so many nurses that gave so much of themselves for soldiers injured or maimed on the battlefield. So many true instances of soldiers falling on grenades to save their buddies. I personally know of several true stories of men who risked their lives under intense fire and pressure to save a wounded buddy or carry his lifeless form to a safe LZ to be choppered out and not left behind. It is well acknowledged that a primary motive for fighting in intense combat is pure love for friends and a desire to protect them personally. This is a far greater motive even than love of country, the flag, and protection for our families back home.

Even today, these many years later, there is so much love shared and joy gained in reuniting with those who were there, those with whom we share so much, those we cared about so much then and still do. That bond will never be broken. We grieve when we lose one, whether through Agent Orange cancer, through suicide, or through natural causes. We rejoice when one is healed of his PTSD. We celebrate when we see a donut dolly at a reunion or at a war memorial. We have great fun telling old stories of the good stuff, the memories of the times that were so positive: going on a MEDCAP to help heal the villagers, taking a hot shower outdoors in the jungle at the end of the long, sweaty, dirty day (the water was hot because we left the five gallon cans out in the sun all day), griping about being put on the s—t burning detail again (mixing diesel with the "stuff" to burn it—the Army sewage disposal system in the field). By the way, we always avoided walking through the smoke. You can see why. Can't you?

All this is a form of expressing love. The bonds are tight among those who went and served under fire. After all, even Jesus said in the Holy Bible, "Greater love has no one than this, that one lay down his life for his friends" (John 15:13). Jesus laid down His life for you and me. Many of our buddies laid down their lives. This love is powerful stuff. It reaches out to us even today. God reaches out to heal us now and forever. We reach out to each other now, as we did then. Then it was to save a life or to help a buddy. Today it is still to heal a life, to help a buddy. We reach out to just enjoy life a little more because of the power of what happened then and the meaning it brings now when we share it. This is love in action.

Let me close off with another word from the Bible. Jesus said, "You shall love the Lord your God with all your heart, and with all your soul, and with all your mind. This is the first and great commandment. And the second is like it, you shall love your neighbor as yourself" (Matthew 22:37-39 RSV). Love is what it's all about.

Margaret, you may have only been a dog. But you were someone's pet. You were important. So was Charlie Chicken. You taught us a whole lot about love. Our love and God's love. May we never forget.

5

medcaps

MEDCAPS AND MY LAI. WHAT DO THEY HAVE IN common? Nothing. Absolutely nothing. OK, they both begin with the letter M. They both involved American soldiers in Viet Nam. But you know what I mean. One is good. Completely good. The other is bad, 100 percent bad. So they have nothing whatsoever in common, regardless of what the media and the movies would have you believe. If you saw *Born on the Fourth of July* or if you read some of the other stuff the media put out, you could get a real complex. Sure, I've read a lot about My Lai. It was an unspeakably rotten, abhorrent thing for our side to do. No rational person would deny it. But it wasn't normal. It wasn't how we believe in treating people, how we fight wars or how we do anything else. There was no excuse for it, even considering adrenalin charges, rage, and how men react under combat pressure. I also know that it was an American helicopter crew that came along and helped stop it from getting worse than it was. They intervened at the risk of their own life and health.

Regardless that it happened, My Lai was an aberration. It was abnormal. Even in that dirty war, it was not what America stood for. It was not how we operated. Not ever. It violated everything noble and right that we were there for. It also violated what our buddies and brothers gave their lives for in that faraway place. We didn't get away with it, either. It haunts us to this day. Let me say one more thing about My Lai and then I'll move on to something a lot happier. If My Lai had been normal, you would have never heard about it because it would not have stood out for the media to notice and report on, as if it were an everyday thing. It stood out because it was so horrifying and so alien to everything we have ever stood for as a God-fearing nation with high moral, human, and spiritual values.

There are a lot of ways to prove the point. Orphanages, kids running up to tanks in jungle villages for the candy they knew soldiers would give them, POWs who weren't tortured when we took them in, and old women who smiled when our tanks, ACavs, and howitzers roared through their villages. These things proved the point of who was the good guy and who was the bad guy. Don't get me wrong, we did plenty we need to repent of. I've talked about that. But our guys still weren't the baby killers, pillagers, and rapists that some want you to believe.

Remember MEDCAPS? Of course, you do. You probably went out on a few. So did I. MEDCAPS were what we did normally. Our troopers wanted to do them. At least the ones I rode with did. If you want to look at something that represented who we were, why we were there and what sort of people Americans were, even in the jungles of Viet Nam in the middle of a messy war, then look at MEDCAPS. MEDCAPS were regular activity. Blackhorse troopers liked MEDCAPS. Maybe there were a few who didn't, but I never met one like that. And I went on plenty.

We went out on one MEDCAP to a Montagnard village somewhere on the edge of the jungle between Loc Ninh and the Cambodian border. Some of our guys set up the ACavs as a perimeter for security while our medics and whoever else set up a makeshift clinic in a shady area. It was a great little village. The bamboo huts were built up on stilts so the pigs, dogs, and chickens could have a place to scratch around, sleep in the shade, and stay out of the house. Little kids ran around naked or with just a shirt and no pants on (very practical for busy mothers). The people came and got shots, pills, and medicine. And, of course, just like back home, the little kids got a Band-Aid for their scraped knees. Were they proud of their Band-Aid? You better believe it. Just like you were when you were a little kid and Mom would give you a Band-Aid. It sure made your knee better. Vietnamese little kids were just the same. Even in the jungle. Remember? You guys were the ones who did it. Be glad. Be proud.

I remember another MEDCAP. This one was in the jungle somewhere in a Montagnard village too. I don't remember just where. Sorry. I don't remember which recon troop I was out with that day, either. But I do remember a couple of things about it. One was that a bunch of old folks were sitting on a bamboo platform having a mid-afternoon party. Half their teeth were gone and the ones that were left were black with beetle-nut juice from years of chewing and spitting. They were having a great time. No wonder, they were getting loaded on rice wine. Remember their rice wine? I expect you do. It was almost pure alcohol!! It looked like white lightnin' from the hoots and hollers of old Appalachia. They were drinking out of glasses that were black with smoke or something—I don't even know what. They invited us to join their party. Here's where my memory gets fuzzy, and not from any booze either. I just don't remember our guys drinking any and it wasn't from being teetotalers. It was just from the looks of those glasses and the foul smell of that "wine." I'll admit that the "ambiance" didn't help. (Look that up in the dictionary.)

My other memory of that MEDCAP was that the people our medics treated had pretty severe burns from a VC attack the night before. Who do you think these people feared and who do you think they trusted? I never heard of a VC or NVA MEDCAP. Anyway, I'll never forget one of the burned villagers. It was a young woman with her baby. Both had been burned. They were OK, walking around and such. The medic put salve on the baby's burns, which pleased the mother, naturally. Then he put some on the mother's burns too. Now, you have to remember that Montagnard women didn't generally wear tops. It wasn't part of their culture. The girls only covered their breasts when American GIs came through ogling them. But no one was ogling these women. Our guys were treating them with the greatest respect. Even the medic treating this mother whose breast had been burned was treating her very gently, professionally, and with complete respect. I was proud and the villagers were grateful. Remember? The guys who I'm talking about might be reading this even as we speak. Thanks, men, if you're there.

Like I said before, our side wasn't always squeaky clean by a long shot. I could tell you stories of things our own people did that I was ashamed of and I expect they are too. Now, if not then. You have your own stories. We've talked about these things before and we will again. But now we're talking about our good side. And I want to make a point very clear that all this good stuff and virtue on our side as Americans didn't just come out of thin air. Having these values didn't just happen. The good and noble side of what we Americans in Viet Nam stood for and fought for came from our heritage. These values and virtues came from a foundation of principle and a strong belief in God and the Judeo-Christian worldview handed down by our forefathers. A high view of human life doesn't just happen. Psalm 33:12 says, "Blessed is the nation whose God is the Lord." I guess you know what our American national motto is. It's on our coins. It's "In God We Trust." That didn't come out of thin air. It's our national heritage too. It's what this nation was founded on. It's a lot of what motivates us. We, as Americans, are truly blessed of God. It's this heritage that makes us what we are and drives so much of what we do.

The Puritans came over on the Mayflower. Then a lot of other people came on more boats (OK, "ships" to the Navy).

They brought a strong belief in God with them. They knew Jesus Christ as the Son of God and just felt like worshiping him without the government telling them how to do it. They weren't perfect either. But they did know what they believed, and that was that God is God and that people are of infinite value and deserve to be loved and respected. And that, in a nutshell, is the heritage handed down to us in our own day. That's why we treated people properly, so far as possible in the context of a war that we believed was just. That's why even to this day the Vietnamese people on the streets of Saigon and Loc Ninh will smile and be friendly when they find out you're an American and not a Russian. Even the Montagnards, Cambodians, and Vietnamese knew what we stood for. For that matter, even the VC and NVA knew what we stood for. Maybe we'll talk about that sometime. That's why we built schools. That's why we built orphanages. That's why we were there to begin with.

That's why we did MEDCAPS.

6

call signs & handles

"BATTLE 6!!, BATTLE 6!!, BATTLE 6!!" CAME EXCITEDLY over the TOC radio one bright and hot day in the jungles of Viet Nam. We were set up at our FSB along QL14 between Loc Ninh and Bo Duc/Bu Dop. I was standing there by the map board with the S3 air and whoever else was in the TOC at the time. The Ole Man, our squadron commander, had just taken fire in his Huey command helicopter flying at about 500 feet over QL 14. He was coming down from visiting F Troop. I believed then, and still believe now, that he was one of the best squadron or battalion commanders in the U.S. Army at the time. Those dinks should never have shot at him. They put a round through the floor of that helicopter that went right between the Ole Man's feet. He got so "excitable" that he was calling his own call sign. Battle 6 was his call sign. When he realized what he was calling he changed it to the TOC call sign, the S3, or whoever it was he wanted to get the action he was after. They proceeded to make those dumb VC sorry they'd ever thought of shooting at our CO.

Whenever I think of call signs I remember that incident. It was funny in a way but it was serious in a much bigger way. It was funny to hear our CO calling his own call sign. But it was dead serious knowing what he was after and what he got.

When he got past the hype, which was immediately, he brought skunion upon the heads of those VC. Whoever was at the TOC listening in knew exactly who was talking and what it was about. There was no mistaking who it was. We knew Battle 6 very well, indeed. Know what? Battle 3 also knew just who his call sign meant. It meant S3, the operations officer. Battle 16 knew who he was too, he was the E Troop commander. And Battle 26A knew who he was. He was F Troop first platoon leader. And so forth. If you were a machine gunner on an ACav, you knew which track was being called because you had a call sign and you knew what it meant when the commo came.

Call signs had a precise and important function. It was to identify the officer, NCO, or trooper occupying an exact position within the organization. When the call sign came over the radio or you were referred to by call sign at a meeting you knew just who was being talked to. Identification was not a problem. That was *you* if you held that position. If you left, PCSed, went on R and R or whatever, then someone else took the position. It wasn't the name of the person that counted, it was the position. I was Battle 11. I don't know why I got eleven, but I knew who was being talked to when my call sign was used. Maybe your job didn't call for a specific call sign of your own. But you still knew you were included when your personal leader's call sign came over the net. So call signs took in everyone. No one left out. Remember? Do you remember yours?

These call signs were very useful, of course. After all, that's how you communicated. Names were funny over there in Viet Nam. Many of the guys had handles, which you surely remember. I won't talk about that here except to remind you that it was a regular way of communicating in those days. You might not have known your buddy's real name but you knew him real well by his handle. You probably remember a lot of handles. You probably remember a lot of call signs too. You heard them enough. Like in a firefight you'd hear the troop commander or the platoon leader or platoon sergeant's call sign hollered back and forth for support or giving fast and frequent sitreps. Your life depended on understandable and clear communication. Call signs did that. When you wanted the leader, you didn't care what his mama named him when he was born, you wanted to say something to him about what he had to do because of his job right now. The call sign made that connection. When you had to have ammo, you talked to Battle 4. If the water came out to the field contaminated with diesel you got on the net, got ahold of Battle 4 Rear and gave him the what-for. Remember? How could you forget?.

Call signs changed from time to time. You probably remember that too. I think mine went from Battle 11 to Workhorse 11 or something. I'm not sure. My memory is foggy now. After all, it's been way over thirty years and I feel pretty good just remembering one squadron handle/call sign for sure and that was Battle. I realized we needed to change for security, though. After all, the VC weren't always as dumb as the ones who shot at the ole man's helicopter that time. They would listen in and learn pretty fast what our call signs meant. Then they could interpret what was going on. That was to our detriment, of course, which was opposite to what we needed. So we changed call signs from time to time. It was to confuse the VC (and NVA, of course) and not us. It worked pretty well, as far as I know. At least most of the time.

I'll tell you about my original call sign. It's one I still use when I e-mail people. I don't have any good reason except I just like doing it. It brings back old memories, good memories, mostly. Maybe that's because I liked the guys who tagged it onto me. It's probably about the same way you got your handle too, a handle being a personal call sign. Mine was acquired like this: My first tour in Viet Nam was down in the Delta at Soc Trang. It was the southernmost American installation in Viet Nam except for an advisory team south of us. We had two companies of assault helicopters, the Mekong

Delta's medevac helicopter company, and a company of Bird Dog fixed-wing spotter planes plus everything that went with them on that little airfield. It used to be Japanese, then became French in the days before we came. My first day there I walked into the club since that's where we ate our meals, including the pilots. The bar was there too, of course. So when I walked in, the pilots started calling me "Sin 6." Well, I have a sense of humor too. So I said, "Hey"(or "Hay"), I'm not in charge of the sin department. But I'll be in charge of the saint department, if you want. So it stuck. I was called Saint 6 after that. It was just in jest, of course. But it became my call sign. Like being called "Sky Pilot," "Padre," or "Chap." I liked it just fine. Still do.

It may be news to you that God has call signs too. Did you know that? I'll tell you about it. You can check it in the Bible. God goes by many names, all of them expressing an attribute, which means characteristic. This isn't a Bible study so I'll just mention one divine call sign to make my point. God goes by the name of Jehovah, or Yahweh. In the Bible's original language, which is Hebrew, I understand it's spelled YHWH. Know why it isn't spelled out completely? Give up? It's because the Jews of Bible times had so much respect for God that they wouldn't spell out his whole name. It was considered to be grossly disrespectful to do that. I understand that, even to this day, Orthodox Jews won't print the name of God because of their respect for his name, his handle, his call sign. That's profound. Sure is a different world from a lot of people I know who drag God's name through the mud as a normal way to talk. That's in addition to how they ask God to damn everything from soup to nuts whenever his name crosses their lips.

Jesus has call signs too. These are important beyond measure because they are so loaded with meaning for what he is all about. For example, one of his call signs is Christ. Jesus is his name, Christ is one of his call signs. It means he's the Messiah, the Savior. It means he has the divine ability to forgive sins and qualify anyone for eternity in heaven who believes in and commits to him. Or Lord. That's a call sign too, a title and a handle. It tells what place Jesus occupies in the life of whoever believes in him. It means that he is the authority, the guide, the teacher and, voluntarily speaking, "the Boss."

A section of the Bible, written way before Jesus was born, talks about what some of his call signs will be. This'll finish what I have to say for this subject: "For to us a child is born, to us a son is given, and the government will be on his shoulders. And he will be called Wonderful Counsellor, Mighty God, Everlasting Father, Prince of Peace. Of the increase of his government and peace there will be no end. He will reign on David's throne and over his kingdom, establishing and upholding it with justice and righteousness from that time on and forever. The zeal of the Lord Almighty will accomplish this" (Isaiah 9:6-7).

7

except for the war part

DID YOU EVER PLAY THAT OLD PARLOR GAME WHERE someone says a word and everyone else says whatever comes to mind? It was fun was because of all the different associations people have with words. Like one person says, "car!" Quickly someone replies, "Ford!" or "Chevy" or "fast" or "I got a speeding ticket last night" or "How am I going to explain my bashed-in front end." See what I mean? Or someone says, "car!" and it gets more complicated. Like there's a used car salesman in the group and he replies, "honest!" when he's really thinking, "How am I going to sell this high-mileage beast!" Or someone else is a mechanic and says, "fixed!" and wonders how he can get a date with the gorgeous blonde who brought the car in.

Let's take this little game a step further. Let's zero in on a word that'll hit closer to home. It's guaranteed to bring out a lot of different response words and feelings. And memories. Let's try the word. Let's go out to the edge. Let's try *"Viet Nam!"* "Hey!!" (or Hay!!), you say, "What're you trying to pull here, Chaplain?" Whoa. Slow down and come along with me. So, let's try this again: *"Viet Nam!"* Now right away you say words or thoughts that come to mind. For those of us who were there, many come to mind. For others of us who had someone over there, many come to mind, too. Right now we'll talk to those who were there. Everyone else can come along because you were involved too. So here goes: I was there for two tours and a word that comes to my mind immediately is "war." You too? Not hard to understand. What about "shooting?" What about "dinks?" (Not all Vietnamese were dinks—just the ones who were trying to kill you.) What about "getting ambushed," "calling for air support," "seeing the stuff fly," "sappers in the wire and green tracers in the air." These are all words and thoughts that will come immediately to the mind of a lot of us who were there. There are plenty more too. You know what I'm saying—you have plenty of your own. So far these are all bad words and thoughts. Right? Yes. No one's kidding here. You have boucoup (boo-coo, so who can spell in French?) bad words and thoughts about *Viet Nam.* So let's check another angle on that word *Viet Nam.*

Let's go on to the flip side. Everything listed above is about the Viet Nam *war.* Just for the heck (I avoid saying hell because I'm not going there) of it, let's think about Viet Nam without the war part. Go to the good part. I'm nuts, you say? That may be true, but I'm from California and that's beside the point. I don't know what I'm talking about, you say? Well, I was there and I got shot at standing up, lying down, in the air, on tanks, and so forth, too. But, as I said, that's the war part. So let's talk about it *aside from the war part.*

We've talked a couple of times about handles. You know, the nicknames guys gave each other that seemed to fit their personality or situation. You remember that sometimes you knew your buddy by his handle and never did get to know his real name. It wasn't important then. Of course, when you tried to look him up later you had a hard time because you didn't know his real name, his handle wasn't in the phone book and no one else knew who you were talking about. The point is, in Viet Nam there were a few buddies that you went through hell (I'll use the word here because it fits) and high water with and you got tighter than with a blood brother. You'd sit around at night talking about very personal things.

You covered each other's you-know-what when the stuff was flying. You took care of each other. You missed your buddy deeply when he PCSed and went home. See what I mean? This was a powerful and wonderful experience. Many, maybe most, of us will never have that profound bonding with anyone again. Only in the extremes of Viet Nam or somewhere like that could this happen.

Moving on to something lighter but also good, I discovered that almost all American soldiers truly care about people, especially kids. We went out on MEDCAPS, which meant we were taking medical care to people in remote parts of the jungle along the Cambodian border, because that's where we operated. Our medics (who usually had the handle of Doc) treated a lot of people who needed help. The rest of us went along to help pull security or just to be friendly with the people. I've been around hundreds of troopers who went out on MEDCAPS (or supported orphanages) just because they wanted to. I can safely say that most, probably all, actually enjoyed doing it. This was definitely a "good" part of our Viet Nam experience. It's a good memory. It's a positive response when someone plays the word association game that I started this chapter with. The good words, like MED-CAP probably don't come to mind as quickly as the bad words, but they're there and they're important.

I hope you agree that, except for the shooting part and missing your family and home, the lifestyle wasn't so bad. First tour I was with helicopters and Bird Dogs in the Mekong Delta. I got in a lot of hours flying around in helicopters, Bird Dog spotter planes, and Otters. Second tour I was with Cav (*armored* cav) and rode around on ACavs, tanks, self-propelled howitzers, more helicopters and so on. This was actually fun. I enjoyed it a whole lot. Where else could you get such rides and experiences (remember, now, I'm not talking about the war part). I remember when we went into Cambodia (legally). We went in through the Fish Hook, into the rubber plantations around Snoul. It was a remarkable experience because the plantations were fresh and green. The plantation homes were whole. None had been bombed or rocketed yet. That would change (but that's the war part again). Except for the war part it was even fun. The French plantation owners were already gone and the Cambodian manager was on his way outta there. He was flying out in a small plane from the grass air strip. As he was leaving he told our troopers they could have anything and everything because what they didn't take, the NVA would come and take anyway. Remember those old, ugly French Citroens? They had to have been one of the ugliest and cheapest cars ever made. We sure couldn't use them and we weren't going to let the NVA have them. So guess what—our tankers had a field day. They took those ugly Citroens out on the grass air strip and had a demolition derby, M48 vs. Citroen. Tanks won, for sure. No kidding! What fun! What a great time! Where else could you do such a thing? Nowhere.

The good stories are endless. But you get the point— there was a lot of good that's worth remembering and thinking about. We don't always have to concentrate on the bad (the actual shooting part of being in the Nam).

Being a chaplain, some of my memories are about having church in the jungle. The Catholic priest from another squadron and I would get on the helicopter, which the regimental chaplain got from the commander. He'd take us all around to have services. The Catholic would take the Catholics (logical enough) and I'd take the Protestants (logical too). When he was gone I'd take everybody, and when I was gone he'd do the same. Everybody, that is, who went to the services. I'll have to say that participation sure was a lot better out in the jungle than in the rear. That shouldn't be hard to figure. Even when it rained we'd have church. I still have the Bible I used out there. It still has splotches from the rain. I didn't mind. It was even sort of fun. It's a good memory.

There's a lot more we could talk about. You can ponder your own good stories from Viet Nam. Spend some time and energy thinking about buddies and experiences except for the war part. When you do, I hope and trust that you'll think about God too. He was there. He did bring you through. And it wasn't all bad by any stretch. I hope you'll recognize that God does love you and cares about you deeply. He has his own call signs and handles, as you may remember from another chapter. One of these is "God is Love." That comes from the Holy Bible, which is my authority for talking about God. It's in 1 John 4:7-10. The rest of this chapter is important too so I hope you'll read it. If you've gone to sleep, you can read it later. Don't forget. Here it is: "Dear friends, let us love one another, for love comes from God. Everyone who loves has been born of God and knows God. Whoever does not love does not know God because God is love. This is how God showed His love among us: He sent his one and only Son into the world that we might live through him. This is love: not that we loved God, but that he loved us and sent his Son as an atoning sacrifice for our sins" (NIV).

To close off, I'll just say that I recognize war is hell and Viet Nam was no exception. Same for Iraqi Freedom, Desert Storm, Afghanistan, Korea, WWII and the rest. But along with the war part many good things did happen. Even great things happened. I hope you'll think about the good things that happened to you. Even in the Nam.

8

shower buckets, hot chow, and ice

RIDING WITH THE BLACKHORSE IN VIET NAM HAD A LOT of advantages that we often got so used to that I think we took them for granted. What in the world am I talking about, you say? Well, I'll start off by admitting that life was a bit rugged over there, even with the mighty Blackhorse. An understatement? OK. But think about it and reminisce a bit. Of course, we were fighting a war. We got shot at and things like that—even chaplains got shot at. True. Just got in the way, I guess. Just the same, there were certain advantages to being Blackhorse, Armored Cavalry. Number one, of course, we had big guns, lots of ammo, and thick metal ("heavy metal?") to protect against a lot of enemy fire, of which we were the ungrateful recipients (got shot at mucho). There were certain other advantages too. Like shower buckets, hot chow, and ice. Remember what I'm talking about? You do if you've been thinking and reminiscing like I asked you to.

I'll illustrate with a true story. We had the mission of "escorting" a gaggle of Rome plows up QL14 to clear the highway for the Vietnamese. That was so when we left the country they would have their roads back. We did a good job, too, which you know, having been there. But we still needed a little help. That came in the form of a grunt company to cover our flanks. They did that by *walking* through the jungle on our flanks while we *rode* on armored tracks on the road and over the bush and trees knocked down and burned by the Rome plows. I remember (you probably do too) what we used to say about each other. The grunts said they were better off because they wouldn't ride around in those iron coffins fer nuthin'. We said we had it better because we didn't have to walk wherever we went. So I guess we were all sort of happy about our style of life in the jungles of Viet Nam.

However, in addition to not having to walk everywhere we went, we had certain other advantages too: namely shower buckets, hot chow, and ice. A whole lot of other stuff too, like whole cases of soda (beer too, like Carling Black Label—ugh) and C rats covering the floor of our tracks. On top of the cases of ammo, that is. I mention shower buckets because they sort of represented an advantage of Armored Cav in the jungles that grunts didn't have. I clearly remember busting around all day on top of a tank or an ACav. You sure could get dirty (see chapter 19 on "Eating Dirt"). Sure was great to be carrying those five gallon cans of water that the Chinooks (S—- Hooks, you know) sling loaded out in big rubber bladders. If we weren't in a contact or whatever you could hang your shower bucket on a branch, a gun tube or something and take a nice, refreshing shower. Warm too—the cans sat in the sun all day. Of course, there wasn't any privacy to speak of. None to not speak of, either. Actually, if you went behind something to get some privacy so no one could see your bare butt while you showered, some VC would probably shoot that bare butt while you were having your privacy. (Another reason for no females—would have been too distracting—know what I mean? Are you normal?) On the other hand, those poor grunts we were working with usually had to go without getting clean until they came to a river—no pristine lakes available. No wonder they got jungle rot and stuff like that. Not to mention B.O.

Then there was the hot chow. I'll be the first to admit that Cs could get pretty boring. Well, maybe you were first, but I still have to admit it. Cs day after day sure put a stress on the joy of eating. But even you have to admit that we had it made compared to the grunts on our flanks. Like I already said, we had Cs by the case. Grunts had them one at a time, or however many they could carry on their back. We had so much (so many?) Cs that guys would dig through the case, pick out what they liked, and give the rest to mama-sans or baby-sans or whatever sans were in the villages. No wonder Vietnamese in the vills liked us so much. Which they did. [Was your favorite C rat ham and eggs? I doubt it. Probably fruit cocktail or pound cake. Maybe peaches]. Now go beyond C rations. Being Armored Cavalry (the *real* Cav) we got re-supplied every day, all things being equal. In other words, not getting shot at at the time. As I recall it, we usually had a hot meal every day. With exceptions like I just mentioned. That hot chow was usually sling (slung?) loaded out by Chinooks. I haven't even brought up having a cook in the field which recon troops had. At least a lot of the time. I think he usually cooked hot breakfast. Sure had it a lot better than those poor grunts. For them, Cs again. I guess they got hot chow sometimes, but not like us. Good to be Cav, like I said…or like you said too, at the time.

The ice part was pure luxury. Sure good to be Cav. (Am I repeating myself?) Not that we had ice all the time. But even once in a while was just fine. Don't you remember those big blocks of ice with the rice husks still all over them? That's how the Vietnamese kept ice from melting in hot weather. They kept it under rice husks for insulation what with not having any refrigeration like we had at home, back in the land of the big PX. Actually, Americans in the pioneer days kept ice in the summer in similar ways—they cut it from frozen ponds in the winter then packed it in straw in cellars where it would keep for the summer. How's that for interesting? Cool! There are more stories about ice in Viet Nam— you can add your own because I'm getting too long and I have a couple of other things to mention before I sign off.

I'll wind down with a couple of related thoughts. I don't know what time it is where you are, but it's only afternoon here. So bear with me and let your eyes droop later. What these stories about shower buckets, hot chow, and ice point out is the advantage of being in the Cav with the living advantages that went with it. Call them life's amenities. Sounds good. But looking to life on a larger plane is more important. I'm talking about all of life. Everything from now to eternity. More specifically, all of it now and in the future. This comes clear in a Bible verse where Jesus said very clearly about himself, "I have come that they may have life, and have it to the full." That's from the New Testament book of John 10:10. Check it out. It's pretty awesome, to put it in our vernacular (see dictionary). Jesus meant that in our total life he came so we could have our life measured to the max for why we were born and why we're still here and how to get life to the max.

Food for thought: Living in the jungles of Viet Nam had its "difficulties," which you know all about. But we still had it pretty good with lots of advantages. Same with life, which has its "difficulties." You know what I mean. But the mission of Jesus the Christ, the Son of God, is specifically to provide for our soul's salvation, forgiveness, and fullness of life, even considering the difficulties. Some call it abundance of life. That's a good way to put it. It means a lot to me. How about you?

favorite places

WHAT'S YOUR FAVORITE PLACE? PEOPLE ASK ABOUT mine pretty often. What with living full time in a motor home and after spending twenty-seven years in the Army, I guess it's a logical question. The answer is, I have several favorite places. Lake Tahoe, for example. It's a wonderful and majestic place. The Black Hills of South Dakota are a favorite too. That's where I am now as I begin this chapter. I like the beauty here. I also like the Indian (OK, Native American) heritage of this area. (How it became part of this country is another matter.) Maybe my part Cherokee blood explains it, who knows? I spent some time, like six years, in Germany. I guess my favorite place over there is the Berchtesgaden to Salzburg area. The Austrian and Bavarian Alps are magnificent. The towns are full of character, charm, and unbeatable gast hauses (restaurants.) The people were just fine. That must be why it's a big-time resort area.

But, you say, "This isn't a travelogue. If I wanted to know about your favorite travelling places, I'd read the travel section in the paper." OK. Gotcha. So let's get to the point. Which is still about favorite places. But not the travelogue type. Now let's get our memories into gear for a minute. When you were in the Nam what was your favorite place? That's a broad and open question. But think for a minute.

You did have favorite places, didn't you? Like the club in the rear? OK, so you didn't get to the rear. I expect your very favorite place in the whole of Viet Nam was probably at Ton Son Nhut Air Base because it meant you were on the way home. Right? So, next to that, what was your favorite place? I know some who were ACav driver's who wanted to change jobs ASAP. The drivers compartment wasn't everybody's favorite place. You know why. If you don't I guess you weren't around armored cav. Maybe some liked driving enough to take the risks of getting yours when the stuff started flying because the driver was in a precarious position. Know what precarious means? Look it up. Of course, if you were a driver you know. For sleeping, some guy's favorite place was stretched out on the bench inside the ACav. Some liked a cot outside under a poncho. The M88 crew liked it inside their M88 (tank retriever—right?), on the floor.

Well, now, let me tell you about my favorite places. The subject is places for riding. When you went out on an operation where was your favorite place to ride? We all know it definitely was not inside the ACav or tank, if that was where you crewed. Everyone knew that if you rode inside, you were toast in a firefight or ambush. So you rode on top, except when some brass came by. You got inside until the brass was gone then it was on top again. It made common sense. Some didn't have common sense. But you did if you rode on top. I don't remember where the hog crews rode. For the uninitiated, a hog was a self-propelled howitzer, 155mm. Right? But riding wasn't inside, as I recall. Same reason. Except for the driver, of course. Anyway, I don't recall hogs even having anyplace to ride inside. Do you? (Even when the brass came by.)

Let me tell you my personal favorite places to ride. Of course, since I'm doing the writing, I get to do the telling. Naturally, you don't have to listen (or read). But I think telling you about my favorite places will stimulate your memories too. So you can relate. (Some thinkers call that communicating. Whatever.) I'll start with helicopters, which most of you rode in only occasionally or maybe just a couple of times except for the Air Cav Troop guys who rode in helicopters a lot, like every day. Anyway, the Catholic chaplain and I rode them every Sunday. Other days too as they were a very quick way to get around. (Obvious.) My favorite place was on the end seat, buckled in and with the doors off (or just open). That way I could lean clear out and look straight down over wherever we were flying. It was exhilarating and fun. During the week, I spent a lot of time riding around with the recon troops doing things like looking for VC and things like that. It was exhilarating in its own way, especially whenever we found some VC. Same with NVA. I don't think I'd classify it as exactly fun, but it sure was exhilarating. Got your adrenalin pumping. Moving along, my favorite place in (on) an ACav was to ride sitting on the driver's hatch lid. You remember. Since everyone was riding on top, the ACav wasn't closed down. Even the driver had his head stuck out on top. So the hatch cover was laid back and made a great place to ride. Much better than the rear hatch cover which was fine except that I have short legs and kept sliding down. I couldn't get a grip with my feet like I could on the driver's hatch. They (I don't remember who) said a few times that my favorite place was also a great place to get waxed if we hit a mine. But we didn't hit a mine. Thank God. (Literally.) Just got shot at—a separate problem.

Riding on tanks and hogs was a different matter. They had a driver's hatch cover, but it was very hard to sit there. Matter of fact, it was impossible because the main guns on tanks and the tubes on hogs were in the way. And they were more important than someone riding on the driver's hatch. So on the tank I rode on the bustle rack. Or was it the bussel rack? I never did figure out how to spell it. Anyway, it was the cage type thing welded onto the back of the turret where the crew kept all their important stuff like soda and beer and maybe some ammo or whatever. Probably kept ponchos and

the like there too. It was a great place to ride because you
were high up and could see everything. Even when there was
stuff you didn't want to see. Even when you wished you
weren't there at all, like in an ambush. But the fun was the
ride and swinging out over the side when the TC swung the
turret to shoot to the side. Next was the hog. Now that was a
trip. The hog didn't really have any place to ride, which may
seem like a strange thing for me to say. But with no place
built in to ride, the guys fixed me up just fine. They put a
lawn chair on the flat part next to the tube and that's where
I rode. Solid comfort. You may think, "What a strange place
to ride," when you realize I was beside the gun (howitzer)
tube. But they didn't just swing it around and shoot from the
hip like the tanks (including Sheridans) did. So I was safe in
that regard. But it did have its challenges, like not falling off
when the hog made a pivot turn—which happened on the
road from Snoul on the way back into Viet Nam from
Cambodia. Made me want to hang onto something except
there was nothing to hang on to. Fortunately, I didn't quite
fall off along with the lawn chair. Made a more careful man
out of me though. So it was still a favorite place. And I
became a more alert chaplain.

Now here's the transition, so stick with me because
favorite places come in many forms and I want to show you
another of my favorite places. Actually, it's my main favorite
place, better than Lake Tahoe and even better than being on
a Freedom Bird. It's sort of explained in the twenty-third
Psalm, which is one of the best known places in the whole
Bible. It's also a lot of people's favorite place in the Bible.
Here's what it says in the part which my Viet Nam experience
makes me think of: "Even though I walk through the valley
of the shadow of death, I will fear no evil, for you are with
me, your rod and your staff, they comfort me" (Psalm 23:4).
That place has carried me through two years in Viet Nam
and more than thirty years since. That place being specifically in the hands and heart (so to speak) of God Almighty.

Jesus, the Son of God, said it another way when he talked about my favorite place (which is the favorite place of a whole lot of other people too): "Come to me, all you who are weary and burdened, and I will give you rest. Take my yoke upon you and learn from me, for I am gentle and humble in heart, and you will find rest for your souls. For my yoke is easy and my burden is light." That's in the New Testament book of Matthew 11:28-30 (NIV).

Like I said about my favorite places, riding on the driver's hatch, the bustle rack, or just being where I needed to be, I had many profound experiences. A lot were even enjoyable. Through it all I hope my life counted for something. I know I cared deeply for the troops I was there to "chaplain" for. But I know also that it was because of being in my very favorite place in God's hands through faith in Jesus Christ that made it all worthwhile and full of purpose. That applies to my whole life just like it can for your whole life too. Which I hope it does.

So, where's your favorite place? Or should I say, "places?" There are plenty to choose from. I hope that being in the hands of God through faith in Jesus Christ is one. The main one. Numero uno. Got it?

10

map reading

REMEMBER YOUR MAP READING CLASS IN BASIC OR AIT? I remember. Remember the E & E (escape and evasion) course? How could you forget? The NCOs gave you a map, told you the boundaries, took you out in the pitch black of night and told you to find your way home. They also told you there was a swarm of enemy out there in those woods who were out to get you and kill you. In training maybe they wouldn't actually kill your body, but they sure would make you sorry you got caught. Anyway, you took out your trusty map, tried to remember all the lessons the Sarge had tried to teach you and then you headed into the bush. Maybe you made it and maybe you didn't. But if you made your goal, it was the map that showed you the way. Even if you got caught, if you knew your map reading, at least you knew where you got caught. So? Just nice to know where you are when you're miserable.

Now, over in the Nam is where the rubber hit the road—where your skin and your life could depend on knowing where you were. If you didn't know where you were, I guarantee Charlie sure knew where you were. Know what I mean? (You know what I mean.) There was the time up by Bu Dop and Bo Duc at the end of QL14 when map reading was crucial. And I mean crucial as in *very* important. There was whole lot of jungle between those little vills and the Cambodian border. One fine day a big gaggle of the bad guys came charging across the border, through the bush (much jungle) and into our AO. Well, our side just happened to have a helicopter gunship team checking them out. Like shooting, spotting, and such. Unfortunately for our side and almost, but not quite, fortunate for their side, they were able to shoot down the Cobra gunship. Naturally, it hit the ground in their AO, which had been our AO. That's when our side got real, real good at map reading. Number one, the other helicopter heroically went down and rescued the downed chopper crew. Number two, they knew exactly where they were on the map, and exactly where the bad guys were. Number three, they brought skunion down upon their heads in the form of air strikes, gunship runs which I think were Blue Max, and artillery. Then our side went in on the ground and cleaned it up. I think the regimental commander said the score was us 0, them 250, give or take a few (going for *low* score.) Good thing our guys took map reading seriously. Right? *Disclaimer: this story is accurate as best as I remember it after more than three decades.*

Remember grid coordinates? Here's a true grid coordinate story: One day I was out with one of the recon troops. I think Miles Sisson was the platoon leader that day. We were on line in the rubber and supposed to do a recon by fire into the bush (jungle) that started where the rubber stopped. So far, so good. The ARVN artillery with an American adviser had the mission of firing support to soften up what was expected to be a hot area. So, here we are, on line and ready to proceed toward the bush. The ARVN artillery began their prep. First rounds landed OK, just into the bush from where we were. Fine. Then the next rounds landed a bit closer to us. Not supposed to. Then more rounds landed a little closer yet. We got jittery. LT called to the American adviser that rounds were coming our way. Adviser responds, "Roger." Next rounds land even closer. LT calls artillery again reminding them that we are where we are. "Roger." Next rounds land almost on top of us. LT calls back again, "Shut it down." "Roger, shut down." Next rounds land so close the shrapnel is bouncing off our ACavs. Naturally, by this time we are inside and battened down. Fortunately for us (and for them later when we got there), that was the last round. We proceeded with our mission to recon by fire into the bush. Got no return fire. Cong had probably dee-dee-maued out of there. I sure would have if I were them. Later we learned that the ARVN artillery knew map reading quite well. They knew exactly where they were firing. But they had a fire mission into that grid on the map and they weren't going to quit until their mission was *feenee* (finished in pidgen Vietnamese), no matter what. So much for knowing the map. At least, we knew where we were and what we were doing. Same for the ARVN artillery. Problem resolved later, I think.

Map reading stories could go on for a long time. But you get the point. No matter what, it pays to know where you are and how to get where you're going. Also, where you've been. Not just in map reading, either. Same lesson applies to life. A wise guy once said, "In life if you aim at nothing, that's just what you'll hit." I don't know who said it, but he was wise, definitely.

This reminds me of the part of the Holy Bible some call the Roman Road. It comes from verses in the New Testament book of Romans. Like a map, the Roman Road tells how to get to Heaven from here (wherever you are in life). If you'd like to check it out here are the verse references: Romans 3:23, 6:23, 5:8, 10:13, 10:9, 12:1-2. What it boils down to is that God is the Creator and Authority on how to get places in life. Like the Golden Rule, for example. If we treat others the same way we want to be treated, it's a whole lot more likely that we'll be happy with our life than if we mess over other people and expect to have a satisfying life. Or if we're generous with our time and our things, we'll be far happier than if we just stick close to the chest and only look out for numero uno. Comprende? Then there's the big one. It's the one that covers it all. In the words of Jesus: "You shall love the Lord your God with all your heart and with all your soul and with all your mind.... Love your neighbor as yourself." This takes care of your whole life, if you think about it. Even if you don't think about it.

What it comes down to is this: For getting where we need to go and knowing where we are and where we've been, it pays to know map reading. Right? Right. Not that we carry a map around all the time. But we still know where we are, where we've been and, hopefully, where we're going, because we know the way. Not that we *made* the way because we didn't. But we *learned* the map. We learned the way from the map that someone with authority made. Same with life. Only life was made by God. He is the authority and it's the wise person who recognizes that and acts on it.

Now I'm in east Texas. From here I'll head west to Arizona and California with my wife. Later we'll head to Oregon, Florida or wherever we figure to go. I guarantee, I won't hitch the car up to our motor home and just start driving. I'll get out the map. I'll see how to get to I-10 and head out by the map. It works. Without that good ole map, where would I wind up? Who knows? Am I glad I can read a map? You betcha. In more ways than one.

c rations, tabasco, and manna

REMEMBER HOW TIRED YOU GOT OF C RATIONS ALL THE time? Remember how y'all (I'm from Texas now) would dig through a whole case of Cs and keep just whatever you wanted? That rarely included ham and eggs. Soldiers who liked ham and eggs were usually a bit strange, even if likeable and good soldiers. Anyone who liked ham and eggs would probably eat anything, maybe even those Vietnamese eggs with little chicks in them. Of course, Tabasco would help make the ham and eggs a little more palatable if you used a lot of Tabasco and were *really* hungry. For the other Cs, I observed many times that troopers would dig through a case, get what they wanted (mostly fruit cocktail), and trade the rest to the mama-sans who peddled gimmicks and stuff alongside the roads as we passed through their villages.

Digging through the Cs, guys sometimes went for the white bread, the cheese spread, and some sort of meat, pork slices for instance. When you got good and tired of plain Cs, which was most of the time, you (or we, because I learned a couple of things about survival too) would make a stove by taking a C rat can, punch holes around the bottom with a church key (not to be confused with the key which would open the door to a place of worship) and put a heat tab or some C-4 in it (don't breath the C-4 fumes because rumor

61

said it will burn your brain cells—I didn't verify this). Then you would take the white bread and smash it flat. Open the can of cheese spread and put it on the flat smashed bread. Place several chunks of pork slices on it. NOW is the time. Load it down with—you guessed it—Tabasco! Put it on the lid of another C rat can and place that on the can with the burning C-4 or heat tab. When done: Voila! Hot PIZZA!! Remember?

More about Tabasco—it's almost peculiar that something as trivial as Tabasco could become so important. I guess it must have been just as important to soldiers around the rest of Viet Nam too, including the ground pounder infantry, who we shared a lot with. Because after a while troopers invented so many ways to use Tabasco that the company, whatever their name is, published a book of recipes that the soldiers of Viet Nam concocted to make their Cs somewhat "eatable." Did you know that? This is a good memory. It reminds me of other things too. It reminds me of men that I like to think about and associate with and of great families who stood by their men. It reminds me of great women who paid a heavy price at home and great kids who knew what their dads did for their country that wasn't appreciated but who served anyway because it was the right thing to do. Memories include those who came home in body bags, men we honor. Memories include those still unaccounted for, POW/MIA. We don't forget. It's strange what a simple thing like Tabasco Sauce and C ration pizza can remind you of.

It reminds me of something else too. Something even more important, which is possible. What C ration pizza and Tabasco reminds me of is another bunch of people, God's people, in the wilderness of the Sinai, the Arabian Peninsula, over three thousand years ago. Even if so long ago, their memory, their story, is fresh as Pizza Hut pizza right out of the oven (pardon the allusion, but that's what comes to my mind, such as it is!). That story is of God leading his people out of slavery in Egypt into the Promised Land. Trouble is, they were a picky sort of people. They were never satisfied. Due to circumstances which you can read about in the Bible book of Exodus, it took them forty years to get to the Promised Land. Meanwhile, they had to eat. There they were in a barren desert, the whole lot of them. As I recall, there were six hundred thousand men plus women and kids. Without a McDonald's or Booger King. What was even worse, almost a catastrophe, there were no C rats and no Tabasco, which hadn't even been invented yet. Too bad because it might have stopped a whole lot of griping. Their griping reminds me of soldiers griping about Cs. Namely the food was boring, boring, booooorrrring. And *bland.* Enter Tabasco. But for the Israelites the food wasn't C rations. It was manna. What? Manna. Say that again? MANNA. What's manna? Look it up for yourself. Like I said, it's recorded in the Bible book of Exodus. Look up Exodus chapter 16 and verse 31. It says, "The people of Israel called the bread manna. It was white like coriander seed and tasted like wafers made with honey." Anyway, the Israelites got sick and tired of manna. Something like GIs got tired of Cs. You can thank the Lord you're an American and not an Israelite. You got Tabasco. They didn't.

A point of this story about Cs, Tabasco and manna is that, even over in the jungles of Viet Nam and Cambodia, even out in the deserts of Arabia and the Sinai, God looks out for us. Especially as we keep our hearts and minds on him, he takes care of us. You know, a lot of GIs didn't exactly live godly lives, even in the Nam, same as a lot of Israelites didn't exactly live righteous lives themselves (and they had Moses to lead them, which was better than a chaplain). But God took care of them anyway, just because he wanted to. He loved them and had a purpose for their lives. Same with us. God loved us in Viet Nam and he loves us now. Maybe you know that and maybe you don't. Maybe you feel that and maybe you don't. Maybe you think you deserve that and maybe you don't. Fact is, no one honestly *deserves* God's love and care. We have God's love and care simply because he wants us to have them. *So we have them.* What I am saying, in case you find this hard to believe or comprehend, is that God loves *you*. Don't take my word for it. Who am I? Just me, and I'm not God, although I do know him. A lot of people know him. A lot of Viet Nam vets know him. A lot of Nam vets' wives and families know him. So now, for the sake of redundancy, I'll repeat—God loves you. God took care of you. God took care of me. Laugh if you want, think me strange if you want, but C Rat and Tabasco pizza reminds me of God's care too. Lest you think I'm really simple, and even if I am, I'll say also that God took care of our buddies, even those who didn't make it. Their problems are over. Their lives weren't long, but they were quality—and that counts a lot more than how many years you get.

I'll close with a verse from the New Testament part of the Bible. It's a quote from Jesus Christ, the Son of God. Don't forget, he went through a lot himself and knows what he's talking about: "Are not two sparrows sold for a penny? Yet not one of them will fall to the ground apart from the will of your Father. And even the very hairs of your head are all numbered. So don't be afraid: you are worth more than many sparrows." This is a quote from Jesus' words in Matthew 10:29-31. If this quote doesn't make much sense, give it a little more thought. A sparrow is about as common a creature as can be found anywhere on earth. But God even knows about them. Regarding the hairs on your head, I don't know how many hairs there are there—there are a lot fewer on mine than there were in Viet Nam days. But God even knows and cares about every one of them. Said another way, God knows the details of you and your life. And he cares anyway. Jesus said God loves you. Take my word for it. Take your buddy's word for it. Take your wife's or your kid's word for it, if you have a wife or kids. But mostly take God's word for it. Because it's true. You can live your life on it.

12

dirty words

(DISCLAIMER: SOME OF THE LANGUAGE IN THIS CHAPTER has been modified, disguised, greatly abbreviated, or had initials, blank spaces, or beeps substituted in order to protect the ears of the innocent and naive or to just keep my computer from burning up…also to help some of you to keep your wife, kids, and mother from knowing how you really talked when you were being uncivilized in the Nam.)

In Viet Nam there were three things that flew freely. Everywhere you went these things were in the air. One was bullets. One was helicopters. The other was the F word. You know all about them, including the F word. Now there are also the S word, the A word, and all sorts of other "words." Saying the letter instead of the word when in mixed company seemed like the polite thing to do. Not that it's anything to be proud of. It isn't. But it was better to use the letter in polite company than to use the word. At least that's the way it was when we were young. Even the men who used it freely, especially in Viet Nam, felt that way. Now it's used way more commonly, even in mixed company. Which is a commentary on how things have changed. But that's another subject for another day.

Back to flying freely—bullets were for dodging, as in get out of the way, unless you were doing the shooting. Then it was let the other guys do the dodging. Helicopters were for catching, as in get on board when you needed to go somewhere, especially out of the jungle for R and R or to finally catch the Freedom Bird back to the world and home. The F word was for talking dirty and not using a clean way of expressing yourself. Of course, it wasn't only the F word. That letter represented a whole sinkhole of expressions that really were pretty foul (not fowl as in chicken; but foul as in stink). Many guys had a lot going on inside them in that combat environment far from home, mom, apple pie, and drag strips. I think young, stressed minds talked dirty partly to just get a lot of the "stuff" (S word substitute) out of their systems; also to be one of the boys, which they thought was very important. In many ways it was *very* important.

That language also was symbolic of things many soldiers did not want to bring home with them. I think there was a lot they did not want to bring back home. I remember specific conversations among troopers I knew and liked very much. They were great soldiers. They were great Americans fighting for their country. Some were loving husbands. Most were single but looking forward to being loving husbands. They wanted to be different when they got back home than they were over there. Survival, being away from home, getting tight with fellow warriors under hard circumstances, living with frequent adrenalin rushes from sudden bursts of energy, fear, and tension during a contact followed by long bouts of boredom and homesickness; all these things and more brought on values and behavior that no one would ever want to bring home. A lot of this was represented by the F word. Some of the conversations I remember included such statements as, "G… D…. Man, I gotta stop this Sxxx. If my ole lady caught me saying such xxxx she'd have my A…" Or, "J…. C…., Man, I can't go home and talk this Stuff (S word substitute) in front of my mom (dad, sister, little brother, girl friend, or whoever)." Troopers also did not want to take home the fear, the hate, the defensiveness, the dirt, the noise, the death and pain, the blood and sleepless nights, the tension. They wanted to go home the same way they came: cool, maybe a little nervous and scared, idealistic, smart-a—ed, maybe, but mostly innocent and worldly *un*wise. So the F word represented a lot of things. I think a lot of men thought that getting rid of the F word when they went home on the Freedom Bird would be a cleansing and maybe represent a return to the way things were before they went. But, of course, that did not happen.

Nothing would ever be the same again. Good, bad, or neutral isn't the point. Boys went over as boys and returned as men. Boys joined the Army to become men. Then they went to Viet Nam and found out more about being a man than they expected. All went over with ideas of what the real world was and found out that the real world isn't just fast cars, pretty girls, getting out of high school, and looking for a job. We found out the real world has an ugly side. But we found out there was something we could do about it too, even if it wasn't much on a historical scale. We found out that we could get real tight with other men in a masculine way, looking out for each other's survival and well-being in the toughest circumstances. We found out what our limits were. We didn't always like what we learned, but we were sure better off for knowing, because we also found out that we had more going for us than we had thought. We also found out what we could take, what we could not take, what we could handle and what we just stuffed ("It Don't Mean Nuthin'"—remember?).

So we mostly put the F word behind us along with what it meant. We also found out it really was different when we got back to the world. *Very* different. (No S...!). Most of us found our place, we adjusted, and got on with our lives. We weren't the same. The world wasn't the same. So what? (No big deal—yeah, sure). But we got on with life anyway. Trouble was, for many the F word hung on and dogged our footsteps. What it meant kept at us. There were the flashbacks, the dirty little secrets, the looks of fear and horror, the loud noises, and all the other stuff I don't need to say because you already know. Too much of what we took on over there still haunts us—the values, attitudes, habits, or just some memories we hate.

We need a fresh start. Even after more than thirty years we need a fresh start. If we are about to blow our stack, we need a fresh start. Even if we're OK, well put together and running our own business, we sometimes need a fresh start. Does this sound ridiculous? Does this sound like just so much religious bull roar (substitute for b... s...)? Does this sound like something from another planet? Does this sound like a bunch of nonsense or something fine for the other guy but sure not for me? Are you hopeless? (Now it's my turn to say, "Bull Stuff.") Hopeless is an attitude and attitudes can change…. Excuse me, I get redundant sometimes. So, for the sake of redundancy, I say again, "*Hopeless is an attitude and attitudes can change.*" Yours too. Comprende?

Now I'm going to introduce a word that you may or may not be familiar with. Maybe you've seen it other places. But it fits here. That word is *grace*. I know it can be a woman's name. But not here. According to Webster's dictionary, grace is God's favor given to us when we have done nothing to deserve it—because we can't do what it takes. It means God's influence acting within us to make us morally strong and eternally secure, which is way beyond what we can do by ourselves. I could go on for a very long time about grace, but I don't want to bore you, even if it is interesting and we need plenty of it. But I'm sure you get the idea.

I'll wind down by quoting three verses from the old hymn, "Amazing Grace." It was written around 1790 by John Newton. He'd been the captain of a slave ship and was so vile a man that even his crew was going to throw him overboard. Then he met Jesus Christ, got saved, and experienced God's grace and forgiveness. So Newton knew what he was talking about when he wrote these words: 1. "Amazing grace! how sweet the sound—That saved a wretch like me! I once was lost but now am found, Was blind but now I see. 2. The Lord has promised good to me, His word my hope secures; He will my shield and portion be As long as life endures. 3. Thru many dangers, toils, and snares, I have already come; 'Tis grace hath brought me safe thus far, And grace will lead me home."

This grace worked for John Newton. He got his fresh start because he accepted God's grace. It had nothing to do with deserving it or earning it. He was the vile captain of a slave ship, remember? He was a drunk too, for that matter. But that all became history because he accepted God's grace. It's worked for believers throughout history. It works for vets as well as anyone else. Nam vets included. It can work for you. "No K...." (That means no kidding, a substitute for another way of talking.)

praying in the rain

I THINK MOST PEOPLE PRAY. I KNOW THERE WERE A LOT of soldiers who prayed, especially when they weren't too sure about their immediate survival. Like when the "stuff" was flying in the jungles of Viet Nam and Cambodia. They weren't thinking about too much theology or formal religion, either; just about "help me get out of here, pleeeeze!" Preferably in one piece. I like to describe prayer as a two-way conversation between a person and God. It happens in a lot of ways and places, one of which I just said. Sitting or kneeling, walking or standing, crouching or ducking, we talk out loud or we talk quietly in our hearts (especially quietly in our hearts if we're out on patrol and you-know-who may be nearby just waiting to blow you away). We believe God hears, then we are quiet and listen to Him respond. We can listen with our ears, eyes, hearts, or our heads. That is prayer. I'll tell you about the memorial service at our Viet Nam vets reunion in New Orleans to show you what I mean.

First, let me be clear that praying for the weather can be tricky. For example, one person might want a perfectly clear day for the beach while a farmer over in the next county might pray for rain because his corn crop is about to dry up. But our experience at the memorial service involved the weather so that's what I'll tell you about.

As a chaplain I've taken a lot of ribbing about the weather. I don't know who Patton's chaplain was at the Battle of the Bulge, but I understand he prayed for good weather on the main day and got it. Because of that, our side was helped a whole lot to win the battle and eventually, the war. Believe it or not, I understand that Patton gave the chaplain a bronze star medal. True story? I think so as it came from a reliable source. I hear about it all the time. I know that I've prayed for a lot of weather in my time and I've gotten some good days—including in Viet Nam and Cambodia. But I never got any bronze star. Just a lot of flack if it rained (good natured flack, of course). Anyway, at our memorial service rain played a very important part. I had prayed for good weather. We almost always have good weather for the memorial services. Hot maybe, but good. But from the way it turned out this time, I think God must have had a good laugh.

We took two river boats down the Mississippi to the place called Chalmette where the Battle of New Orleans was fought in 1814. Andy Jackson was the general and was very popular because we won. If we had lost, I guess we'd still be British. But we won, so we're American. I'm glad. Anyway, I got there a little late because I was on the second boat by mistake instead of the first boat. About eight hundred people were there, the color guard was there, the wreath was in place, the Louisiana National Guard head general was there, and the band was playing. Great. All I had to do was start and everything would just fall into place. So I thought. Only one little glitch. Even though the band was great, the bandmaster hadn't been briefed and didn't know what to do.

We were on a tight schedule because the boats were waiting to take us back so they could pick up their next load of tourists. We barely had time for the service as it was and there wasn't time to coordinate what I thought was already done. The band was playing, the buglers were ready to bugle, the singer was ready to sing, the general was ready to be introduced, the governor's rep was ready to present a citation, my memorial message was ready to go, the cannon to fire, and taps to tap. Except the band needed to know what to do, like I said.

About the time I realized there wasn't time to do all this and coordinate the band too, guess what happened. It hadn't rained all day. It hadn't rained the day before. It didn't rain again until the next day. But it sure started raining *right then*. It started with a sprinkle. No problem. Then it started pouring down—like a Viet Nam monsoon! The band was heroic, but finally had to pack it in. Some people found shelter, but most of us just got soaked. Like Viet Nam. About the time the band got packed, guess what else happened. Yep. It just *stopped* raining, like on cue. And it didn't rain again. Matter of fact, the sun came out. We went on with the service. Everyone had a very meaningful time. All went very well, including the young woman who sang "The Star Spangled Banner" without the band. That ten-minute rain actually added to the service because it was so much like Viet Nam— no big deal.

This was definitely a small thing in the overall scheme of life. No one would write home about it. But it was important anyway. Because of how it happened, the timing and all, I truly believe that God was in the act of answering prayer. We were extremely disappointed at first. Then everyone could see that the rain was OK and we even enjoyed it. What does this have to do with prayer? Well, I asked God to help me minister, didn't I? Yes, I did. And he did. That rain added a touch of Viet Nam. It didn't hurt anybody. The timing was just as if it were scripted. I didn't pray for it to happen that way. God just answered in a way that was better than I asked for. He answered in his way because he cared. And by not having the band play during the service, we were able to keep it short enough so the boat captains wouldn't get mad and leave us.

God really does care about every one of us. That's right, *"God really does care about every one of us."* He cares enough to hear when we pray and to respond in love for our good. We can all tell about memories of Viet Nam, Cambodia, and plenty of other places too. Through good times and bad, tough times and easy, boring times and exciting, with and without our buddies or our families, we know of many times when God showed that he does care now *and did care then.* He did hear our cry. He did bring us through. He still will. He still does.

I'll close off by quoting Matthew 6:25 in the Bible, which is the Word of God: Jesus said, "I tell you, do not worry about your life, what you will eat or drink; or about your body, what you will wear. Is not life more important than food, and the body more important than clothes? Look at the birds of the air; they do not sow or reap or store away in barns, and yet your heavenly Father feeds them. Are you not much more valuable than they?" *Yes. You are.*

You are valuable to God. Through Jesus Christ, his Son, you can pray to Him. Do it. Pray to Him. He cares. He hears. He answers. Sometimes in ways we wouldn't even think of. Like rain when you need it.

14

partners

THE BLACKHORSE REGIMENT HAS PRODUCED MANY heroes in its time, many great leaders, many warriors worthy of great honor. 1SG/Rev. Vernon Nevil was one of them. This chapter is my tribute, my offering of honor, memory and respect for the man who was my partner in ministry with the 11th Armored Cavalry Veterans of Viet Nam and Cambodia since its beginning. Such an individual I have not known before. Probably never will again. Such men God creates and then throws away the mold. I have known many great first sergeants in my twenty-nine-year military career. I have known many great chaplains as well. Rarely have I known a man who combined both into a single person. You simply do not run into a first sergeant/chaplain every day, especially a great one. When I met Vernon I knew I had met one of the rare, one of the great.

We met and ministered together at our first reunion in Dallas. The year was 1986. Vernon and Monna were there. I drove down from Texarkana. They drove up from Marion, Indiana. The next year my wife and I went to the reunion in Washington, D.C. and The Wall. Vernon and Monna were there too. As a matter of fact, Vernon came to every reunion except two. One year he stayed home because of some serious family business which he told us about. The other time was Vernon's last reunion, which was in New Orleans. He couldn't be there that time because he was fighting his war with Agent-Orange-induced cancer. Vernon was *always* with the troops, one way or another. In the jungles of Viet Nam his soldiers knew him to be a firm but fair leader. They knew he saved many lives by his heroic actions under fire. Indeed, Vernon's great respect was earned the hard way among his soldiers. When he wasn't with us physically he was present in heart and spirit. He loved trooper veterans and would do anything for them. He was a mature and secure person who knew who he was before God and before his fellow man. He had his values straight—he was modest in his material possessions but enormously rich in the love and respect of family and friends alike. As a matter of fact, it seems to me that he was modest about everything—unusual for a man of such remarkable ability and characteristics of a real man. Vernon was indeed a man among men as well as a man of God. He would have said being a man of God comes first always and without question.

At the reunions we talked, planned, and had fun while we ministered and shared the chaplain things. We supported each other while we looked out for the troops as best we could. Vernon was a partner one could be comfortable with. At the fourth reunion we were even co-recipients of the Trooper of the Year award. I tell you this so you can see how great Vernon was in partnering and where his heart was. I don't say this about every person I've ever teamed up with, believe me. A quick story: I think it was at the Indianapolis reunion (or was it San Antonio?) where we went downtown to the Veterans Memorial which was in a park a few blocks from the reunion hotel. Everyone was standing around talking and not sure what to do. Vernon reverted back to his first sergeant days, let out a *loud* bellow (you old troopers know what I mean) and definitely got everyone's attention (!!). Then we began the memorial service. That was in the early days when we weren't as well organized as we are today, but we sure had a good time! And the memorial services were appreciated just as much then as they are today. Just not as organized, like I said.

Vernon was a true partner with others too, especially Monna. I want to tell you that it is not every day you see a partnership as close, tight, and harmonious as that between Vernon and Monna, his life's partner and lifetime wife. What a great woman! What a joy to be around! What a special complement to a great man. It looked to me, after only twelve or thirteen years of knowing them, that they illustrated what God meant when He said that a man and a woman should leave their fathers and mothers and become one flesh so long as they both should live. Family members would know better than I, but I believe Vernon and Monna were partnered into "one flesh" in a beautiful manner that is rare in our day. I think it would be rare in any day. They were real role models in a marriage partnership that we all respected completely.

There are several ways Vernon can be described in partnership. Others can and will tell their stories—his wife, his brothers and sisters, his kids, his grandkids, his fellow troopers who fought with him in Viet Nam, and plenty more. There was another partnership to which Vernon was 100 percent committed, to which Vernon had given his life, of which Vernon was not in the least ashamed, and of which he would speak right out, "on top of the table." He had no room for compromising with this partnership and was glad to share it with *anyone*. That was his partnership with his Lord and Savior, Jesus Christ. I have no idea when Vernon accepted Jesus Christ as his personal savior, but he was honest and loving about this relationship. I describe it as a partnership. I think Vernon would approve of me saying it on one condition: that Jesus Christ was the *senior* partner. No messing around about it. Vernon, as many of you know very well, was not one for messing around. Having fun, yes. Messing around, no. Vernon loved the Lord with all his heart, all his soul, and all his mind (and his neighbor as himself—as Jesus Christ said when he was asked what was the greatest commandment). His commitment was so total that he actually went back to school and became a preacher after he retired from the Army. Naturally, he still wore a uniform. Except this time his uniform was bib overalls. A first sergeant/preacher in bib overalls? Yes. From jungle fatigues to bib overalls—you had to know Vernon.

Vernon is in heaven now. He has met his Maker, who I am sure has already said to him, "Well done, good and faithful servant. Enter into the presence of the Lord."

I will finish by quoting a Bible section that was used at Vernon's funeral. He probably said it if he had the time while he was going from here to heaven. It's from the book of 2 Timothy chapter 4, verses 7 and 8: "I have fought the good fight, I have finished the race, I have kept the faith. Now there is in store for me the crown of righteousness, which the Lord, the righteous Judge, will award to me on that day."

God bless you, Partner. Thank you, God, for giving us Chaplain/"Top" Vernon Nevil.

15

i'm 66!

I'M 66! 66 YEARS OLD, THAT IS. NOT 66 IQ. (NO OPINIONS to the contrary accepted). It's a major milestone in my life. Now I collect Social Security. I get into movies with senior discounts. (I've gotten Denny's discounts since I turned 55 and I joined AARP at 50). I'm part of what's being called the Age Wave. I'm a "Senior." I think that's good, considering the alternative (think about it). There were many times I wasn't so sure I'd make it this far. So far, so good.

You see things in a different perspective when you become officially senior. I'm not 30 any more. That's obvious, you say? I know. I see life differently than when I was 30. Although 30 was a memorable year. Why was it a memorable year? It was a memorable year because that's when I was in Viet Nam for my first tour. I was at Soc Trang in the Delta on a small airfield. We had helicopters and Bird Dog spotter planes. That was the year of the Tet Offensive. I went back again later for a second tour. That time with the Blackhorse Armored Cavalry. We went into Cambodia that year. My life hasn't been the same since. Just like your life hasn't been the same since your time in Viet Nam. Our lives have been better or worse, richer or poorer, and different in other ways since then. But not the same

Viet Nam was a defining event for me. It proved something. I don't have it all figured out, but I do know I learned a lot about life and meaning. I learned the hard way…so did you. Whatever else it was, it wasn't an easy way to learn about life. Now I'm 66. Then I was 30 or 32. Over thirty years in between. I've learned a lot during those years too. I went from Viet Nam to Germany, Blackhorse in Viet Nam to Blackhorse in Germany. Cav in Viet Nam to Cav in Germany. Blackhorse along the Cambodian border to Blackhorse along the East German border. Those were the days of anti-war protesters, race riots and inter-racial bashing, beads, hash, LSD, and all sorts of things I could write a book about. Not to worry, I'll keep this short. Going from Viet Nam to Germany in those days, I wasn't sure which was the fire and which was the pot (the kind you cook in). That was a defining event too. I ended up staying in the Army because I liked being a chaplain. I eventually got married and acquired two grandkids (without ever having kids of my own!). That was a defining event! I will let you in on something: I know the pain of divorce too. Married at 40. Divorced at 41. That was a defining event. A hard defining event.

All wasn't hard. Some was great and not hard. I got married again. At 50. That was when I became a grandpa. (That's how you become a grampa without being a pa. Marry someone who already has grandkids!). That was, for sure, a defining event too. I'm still married. Not always easy, but definitely a defining event.

Life keeps moving. Nothing stands still. At 66 I am keenly aware of that. After Army retirement I was a chaplain for a retirement community where the average age was 83. I came to realize that's where I'll be someday. The way time flies, it'll come sooner rather than later. That is, God willing, the Creek don't rise, and I should live so long. Thirty-five years ago I wouldn't have counted on making 66. Now here I am looking at 83. You may not be 66, but your time flies the same as mine.

Why am I saying all this? I'm not saying happy birthday to myself (we did that at Al Capone's old hideaway restaurant near Chicago). I'm saying it because it's so important to live life where you are *now*, not where you were 30 or 35 years ago. I don't always do it so well but I've learned the importance of living my life in the present, looking to the future, and learning from the past. Of course, you can't forget the past. Especially a time as powerful and defining as Viet Nam. I did say it was a defining event, didn't I? That means an event is so powerful that it makes a maximum impact in determining who and what you are. There are other defining events in your life too. Living life in a point of time in the past is getting stuck there. It impedes progress. It ignores other defining life events.

I'm perfectly aware of events that happened in Viet Nam and other wars like Korea, Desert Storm, WWII, Iraqi Freedom, etc. They were traumatic, which is a gross understatement. You know that better than I do. I've talked about some of these things in other chapters. But you have to keep your life moving. If you're stuck at Viet Nam or some other trauma event, get help. There's plenty of help available. If your life is on the move, congratulations! Keep on moving. Use your defining events to make your life better, richer, making progress. Help a brother while you're on the move yourself. It'll make your life even better. Remember to bring your family along. Don't forget the kids. Mostly, don't forget your wife as you move through life. Or your husband (if you're female, that is). If you're not married then don't forget whoever you're close to. Or could be close to if you'd let them in.

There's another defining event to life. Actually, it's the most important defining event there is, Viet Nam included. Matter of fact, this defining event gives sense to the other defining events of life. This defining event provides renewal, forgiveness, and perspective. It brings all these other defining events together, even the traumatic ones. Even the ones which some trooper vets are trying to resolve by moving to the woods. This defining event is God in action.

Now here is where some will automatically go into a thousand-yard stare. This is where some will put this chapter aside. They're the ones who've become comfortable with their misery and don't want to hear a way out. OK. It's a free country. Since it's God we're talking about, I guess I should shut up and let him speak for himself. After all, he's *God*. And, like the kid said, "If there's anyone you want to make happy, it's God." So here's what God has to say about this defining event: "If anyone is in Christ, he is a new creation; the old has gone, the new has come! All this is from God, who has reconciled us to himself through Christ and gave us the ministry of reconciliation: that God was reconciling the world to himself in Christ, not counting men's sins against them. And he has committed to us the message of reconciliation." This is from God's word, the Holy Bible, 2 Corinthians 5:17-19.

I know a lot of vets who think they're locked hopelessly in their Viet Nam defining event. I know a lot of vets who have moved way past Viet Nam and kept up with life but have missed God's defining event for them. I know a few vets who think this is all a lot of…stuff. I know a lot of vets who have accepted God's defining event for themselves and it has changed their whole existence! God gave them direction, purpose, relationships, and cleansing. The cleansing part came through forgiveness, which we've talked about in other places.

I hope all this is clear. Personally, I hope and plan to live a lot longer, God willing. At 66 I've learned things that I sure didn't know at 30 (or 20 or 40). I plan to learn a couple more things before 83. Whether I will actually live that long or not, I don't have a clue. But, if I do, I know there'll be more defining events along the way.

Now, at 66, I've affirmed what I learned years ago, that the *big* defining event to life isn't Viet Nam, it isn't a lot of money or education, and it isn't getting divorced or anything bad. It's accepting a personal relationship with God Almighty through Jesus the Christ, who came just for that very purpose.

Something to think about.

★ 16

short-time calendars

I SOMETIMES TELL PEOPLE THAT I'VE REACHED THE STAGE in life where I keep track of time by decades rather than years. I'm at the point that when I try to remember things that happened, rather than thinking, "What year was that, 1988 or 1989?" I think, "What decade did that happen in, the 60s or the 70s?" See what I mean? I don't know why, but this reminds me of how we kept track of time in Viet Nam. Remember the short-time calendars we used? Of course you remember. Think for a minute, "was it 1966 or 67?" "Was it 1968 or 69?" Or, if you're like me, ask "was it the late 60s or early 70s?" It'll come to you. You couldn't forget if you tried. And why would you try? Short-time calendars were one of the things that kept your head together. Everybody liked them. No wonder. That's how we measured our year in Nam.

There were more kinds of short-time calendars than you could count. Some were funny, some were not. Most were simple drawings you could color in like a kids' coloring book. Some were just wall calendars where you Xed or blacked out each day of the month as you came to it. First thing in the morning, of course, so the whole day would count (or uncount.) The pictures were about almost anything you could imagine. Some soldiers drew their own. Most had mimeographed pictures with the numbered sections already drawn in. (Remember mimeograph?) All you had to do was to fill in the space numbered for the day as soon as you woke up that morning. Some would color each space a different color that made no sense. It was just the color the guy felt like coloring it. Some colored so the picture would come out to be very nice and even artistic. Remember?

*"_Warning_"*The rest of this paragraph is censored so tell your wife to cover her eyes:* Some of the pictures, even the mimeographed ones, were "Naughty Ladies." They didn't have any clothes on. I'll admit, you can't make a mimeographed drawing of a naked lady very graphic, but they got the point across, whatever the point was.

A few of these short-time calendars were by troopers doing real hard time, which I'll explain in a minute. As I recall, just about all the short-time calendars were kept by "short timers." What's a short timer? If you were there, I don't have to tell you. For family members reading this, a short timer was someone doing short time. That means a trooper was short. Has nothing to do with tall versus short. It was a matter of how many *days* a guy had left on his one-year tour. Actually, it was more than that. It was a matter of how many days a guy had left on his tour *and his attitude about it.* Which was being very excited at the prospect of going home to the "real world" but keeping that excitement well at bay (stuffed). That was because anything could happen. Here you do know what I mean what with being in a war and shooting going on all around you, especially out in the bush. Besides, you couldn't let your buddies see you out of control. Anyway, that's what a short timer was. It got more complicated than that, but you can fill in the details.

When a trooper would get his short timer attitude, then he would start his short time calendar. It was a way to see before your eyes that this you-know-what wouldn't go on forever. That there was an end in sight. As I recall, it usually came about the time one would hit the double digits. That

meant he had 99 or fewer days left on his 365-day tour.
Sometimes he would be called a "double-digit midget." "Call
me what you want. I'm short! I can take it." Of course, when
a guy would hit the single digits, 9 or fewer days left, then he
would really start getting serious. Not that anyone was super-
stitious or anything, but just to be on the safe side, the old
man sometimes would let a single-digit midget stay off
patrol and might even give him a rear job. It was a pretty
practical idea. It was always hard when a buddy would get
hit, but it was especially hard on morale when a single-digit
midget got it when he was within sight of going home. I
won't generalize too much. But that's how it was, according
to my memory (which isn't always too clear, but seems OK
today).

I haven't forgotten the hard time I mentioned earlier.
There were a few who did hard time. Good thing it was only
a few. By the way, when I say doing hard time I don't mean
chopping rocks in prison. What I mean is that some guys had
a 365-day short-time calendar, which wasn't short time at all.
It was a calendar where they marked off every single one of
the 365 days of their whole daggone tour in Viet Nam. Every
daggone day in country they thought of going home. That's
what they concentrated on. Some did their job OK but you
might have had to keep an eye on them because their mind
was mainly on when they would get out of there, not on what
they had to do right then and there to stay alive or to help
you stay alive. Maybe I'm overstating this (and maybe not).
But doing hard time sure made the year go a lot slower for
those guys than for the rest who just did regular short time.

Another thing about short-time calendars and being a
short timer is worth mentioning. If it's not really worth mentioning, just chuck this part or go brain dead for a minute
until it passes. That's the part where I think short timer-itis
must have been some sort of a virus. At least it sure looked
like it. I think it was more catching than the flu or malaria
(or some of the other catching things that chaplains aren't

supposed to know about). Some of us, like myself, said we would never get a case of short timer-itis. I'd just do my job until the end and then go home. I thought I'd never start counting the days, not even when I hit the double digits. I suppose this was especially true of soldiers on their second or more tour. Ha-Ha. Bad joke. When I hit the double digits I started counting just like everyone else. I was out of control. I couldn't help it. When you hit 99 it's just too hard to keep from counting. So you start counting (backwards of course): 98, 97, 96, etc., right to the end. And it's impossible to keep from telling everyone around you how short you are. You don't want them to feel bad but, like I said, short timer-itis is contagious. In case you're wondering, no, I didn't keep a short-time calendar of "an undraped lady." Actually, I didn't even keep a short-time calendar at all. But I did catch a heavy dose of the virus, or whatever it was that caused the condition.

And then it was over! That leads to other stories, doesn't it? Makes me think of many, some good, some not good. Like freedom birds, going home, leaving buddies, and such. Makes me think of how all of life goes. After all, these things happened many years ago. Our short-time calendars marked the days and then they were gone! What comes to mind is a section of the Bible in Psalm 103:15-18 which says, "As for man, his days are like grass, he flourishes like a flower of the field; the wind blows over it and it is gone, and its place remembers it no more. But from everlasting to everlasting the Lord's love is with those who fear him, and his righteousness with their children's children—with those who keep his covenant and remember to obey his precepts."

Those days in Viet Nam are still vivid in our memory and in our hearts. But they were a long time ago. Those short-time calendars measured important days that seemed to drag. But now they're history too. Fortunately, that isn't all there is to life. The love of God our Creator is everlasting. Where God is concerned, there are no short-time calendars.

There is no hard time, either. His love has no end. We can count on that. It can change what we are and what we look forward to. Actually, we don't need a calendar at all because living in the love of God is where we want to stay. And we can. We don't ever have to go. It's the *real* real world. Or, like another place in the Bible says, "For God so loved the world that he gave his one and only Son, that whoever believes in him shall not perish but have eternal life" (John 3:16).

Something well worth pondering (you can look *pondering* up in the dictionary).

17

time flies

MOM AND DAD WERE RIGHT AFTER ALL. YOUR MOM AND dad were probably the same as mine. They were always saying how fast time went. Every new year it was the same. Every time something important happened it was the same. "Where did the year go?" "How time flies." I didn't see it that way. I was young and thought time just dragged. I could hardly wait until I was 16 and could get my driver's license. I could hardly wait until I was 18 and could graduate from high school. In Air Force boot camp I thought those interminable drills would never end. Later, with the Army in the jungles of Viet Nam, that year seemed like ten. My first three-year tour in Germany seemed like a lifetime. But, as I grew older, I began to realize that all things in this life really do come to an end. By the time I went back to Germany for my second three-year tour, I knew I should make the most of the time because it would be over with very quickly. I had a lot I wanted to do and needed to become active right away if I was to meet my goals. I kept very busy, the three years went by rapidly, and then it was over. I may never return to Germany. But I'm glad I was able to accomplish most of my goals. It was because I had learned how fast time passes, and I needed to make the most of it while I could.

Now I've reached the stage in life where I tell people that time flies even when I'm miserable, not just when I'm having a good time. Not that I'm so miserable. It's just that time always goes quickly, even when I'm down. You know what I mean. After Army retirement I was a chaplain for a retirement community. Our residents average age was 83. I would hear them talk often about how fast time goes. It's like their whole life has passed in a flash and they were surprised to be where they were. I frequently feel that way at age 66 and counting, which I am now. Mostly counting. How did I get here? Anyway, moving right along, I hear Viet Nam vets talk like that a lot. Other vets too. We meet at reunions. We talk and share. We're excited. Lots of memories—good and bad. Lots of healing. Lots of gray hair. Lots of "spare tires" around the mid-section and lots of follically-challenged scalps. Then it hits between the eyes: it's been a bunch of years since we rode with the Blackhorse. You figure it. It's been the same years since Thunder Run. It's been the same years since we busted jungle or returned fire or hollered "Incoming." Time goes fast. Our whole life goes fast. That's what I think. I think that's what you think too, most of the time anyway.

All this thinking about the passing of time reminds me of something else, a plaque my mother used to keep on top of the television set. We got our first TV in 1952, about the time I graduated from junior high school. The TV was a big deal. Before that we had to go over to my aunt and uncle's house to watch TV. Maybe you remember your first TV. Maybe your folks had it before you were born. Anyway, ours was in a beautiful mahogany cabinet with doors to hide the screen when it was turned off. The plaque sitting on the TV was insightful and thought-provoking. It said, "*Only one life,/ 't will soon be past./ Only what's done/ for Christ will last.*" After all these years I've never forgotten that poem. I have no idea who the writer was, but I am grateful to him or her for penning those important words. The more I get to thinking about time and how quickly it passes, the more I realize just how true the words of that poem really are.

It seems like yesterday that I thought retired people were old. Retirement was something in the far-off future that was only for grandmas, grandpas, and old soldiers, but had no relationship to me whatsoever. It hardly entered my mind that I would ever be one of "them." Now I've been retired from the Army for over ten years and my friend's kids are the same age I was when I was having those thoughts about only grandparents and old soldiers being retired. Now I qualify on both counts of being retired and being a grandpa. Why, I could even be a great-grandpa except granddaughter isn't married and a mommy. Now I realize you don't have to be old to be retired or a grandpa. Or a great-grandpa. Simply amazing!

This reminds me of a scripture that I consider from time to time, "All men are like grass, and all their glory is like the flowers of the field; the grass withers and the flowers fall, but the word of the Lord stands forever" (1 Peter 1:24-25). People are a part of God's creation. Everything goes in cycles: spring, summer, fall, and winter or morning, afternoon, evening, and night. That is the Creator's design. Life is such a wonderful gift of God. Life is full of opportunity, full of beauty and meaning. It is ours to live according to its design and purpose for the time we have it. Of course, life has its trials and tribulations. It has its rocky places and its difficulties. The vet knows this best of all. But, if we will put our hand in the hand of our Creator, if we will trust ourselves to the Risen Savior, then we can look up to see the stars rather than looking down to see the mud. We can see the flowers and the grass rather than the thorns and the weeds. We can see our purpose and our plan rather than drifting aimlessly with uncertainty or futility. Our purpose and our plan are a life-giving force. They include love, healing, forgiveness, atonement, and peace. They are fueled by faith and prayer. They come from God. We talk about these things. We'll talk about them more. They're important.

If you'll notice the grass and flowers scripture I mentioned at the beginning of the preceding paragraph, I'll point
something out for you. The scripture passages that come
before the grass and flowers talk about the positive and powerful: "Now that you have purified yourselves by obeying the
truth so that you have sincere love for your brothers, love one
another deeply, from the heart. For you have been born
again, not of perishable seed, but of imperishable, through
the living and enduring word of God" (1 Peter 1:22-23). I
find great encouragement in these words from the Lord. I
know where I'm headed even though I don't always know
everything along the way. There's an old song that's one of
my favorites: "I don't know what tomorrow holds, but I
know who holds tomorrow."

We are well through this year. We recently passed into
another millennium, hard as it is to believe. Time flies. Time
marks and measures the passage of life itself. I hope that in
God's strength, will, and wisdom, we each make the most of
it, that we even enjoy it. Life is precious. We live it just once.
Then, at the end of the road, we meet our Maker. Through
faith in His Son, Jesus Christ, as I enter the gates of Heaven,
I deeply hope to hear the words, "Well done, good and faithful servant. Enter into the joy of the Lord." I hope the same
for you.

★ 18

lights

"It was a dark and stormy night...." Sound famil- iar? This isn't a mystery story. It's remembering some of the dark-as-pitch nights out in the bush along the Cambodian border, in the jungles of War Zone C, in the Fish Hook of Cambodia and plenty of other places you know about. When you were out there pulling security at night on a hot NVA trail, you sure learned what dark meant. It was dark enough on a moonlit night under three-canopy jungle. But when there wasn't even a moon out, you just had complete dark- ness. It was unnerving. Mostly it was unnerving when you heard strange noises but it was too dark to see, even your nose which was usually in front of your face. Except when it was bent out of shape at something. (Ha Ha. That was a joke. Get it?)

During the day you wouldn't think about light. The sun was plenty bright. Especially in the dry season. But at night in the pitch black darkness, light meant a whole lot. You know just what I'm talking about. I remember one night up near Bu Dop and Bo Duc (which is which, I never figured out). At 0400 I got up to go out to the berm to do what everyone has to do once in a while. It wasn't all that dark. I mean, there was some starlight. Otherwise, it was very dark. Anyway, I was minding my own business when all of a sudden, we got some light! Usually it wouldn't have seemed like much. But under the circumstances it was plenty. What happened was that a couple of trip flares went off right straight out from where I'd been standing at the berm. Someone hollered, "There's two dinks! Shoot 'em!" All of a sudden there was plenty of light. There was light everywhere, piercing the darkness of the night. There were trip flares! There were bullet flashes! There were mortar round impact flashes! There was light from the flares parachuting down above us. Man, there was light all over the place. Good light flashes were us shooting at the bad guys! Bad light flashes were them shooting at us! There was even light from helicopter gun ships. Or maybe they were helicopter light ships. I didn't take time to check exactly. At the first light of dawn it was all over. As the sun came up we were glad for daylight. Then there was a lot to do like medevacing out our casualties and policing up enemy bodies and stuff like Charlie's stashes of mortar rounds. There are times when you become very aware of light. There are other times you don't give light any special notice.

We knew all about nighttime light discipline. On those dark and stormy, or not stormy, nights you could see light, any light, a long, long way off. More than one soldier has made a great target simply by lighting up a cigarette in the middle of the night. Remember how hard it was getting around the NDP in the middle of the night when you couldn't even carry a flash light? If you went out for something, it was almost impossible to find your way back to your track because you couldn't see anything in the pitch black darkness. I, for one, got lost more than once stumbling around in the dark. And I could have been right next to my tent or whatever it was I was looking for. Or should I say whatever I was *feeling* for. Light, any light, was a 100 percent help. Just a speck of light could give you all the bearings you needed to find your way.

One of my embarrassing memories involved a light. A strobe light. Strobe lights are interesting. I don't know who invented handheld strobe lights but they sure came in handy in Viet Nam out in the bush. There was one night when we'd taken some casualties. I think it wasn't too bad, but I don't remember for sure. What I do remember was that I was the one who went into the clearing with the strobe light to guide in the medevac helicopter. That part was OK. No problem. What I get embarrassed thinking about was a very simple thing. Realize, it's often the simple things that get you made dead real quick. This time the real simple thing was that I went out there and stood straight up to hold that strobe light. In that jungle clearing, I was making a perfect target of myself. I was almost inviting any VC who just happened to be passing by to shoot me. Why not? I was there holding the light in the darkness and standing as tall as I could. That wasn't much because I'm not so tall. But I still get humbled thinking about it. In case you ever have to hold a strobe light to bring in a medevac in the middle of the night, always *squat* to hold it. You make a rotten target when you squat. You make a great target when you stand. That's very good advice which you'll probably never need. Oh, well. So much for good advice.

I hope you're not too tired hearing about lights. That's because there was another kind of light out there in the bush of Viet Nam, which I'll mention now. Actually, I suppose there were many other kinds of light out there. But I'm thinking of one other that you're likely to remember. That was the helicopter light ships. Wouldn't you know it, I don't remember just what we called them. But they were Huey slicks with a pod of floodlights in the open side door. The Huey would fly around the jungle or wherever they thought Charlie might be and turn on those lights. I mean to tell you, anyone on the ground would have thought someone had turned the night into day. It was bright. Good for our side because we lit up the night. Bad for the enemy side for the same reason. We made the situation very hazardous for their health and safety. Thanks to the light in the night. Sometimes our side would get in a jam because too many enemy were too close and we couldn't see them in the dark. So we would call in the light ship. Then we could see them which made it bad for them and good for us. They didn't like to be seen. I can understand that. Otherwise, they would have attacked during the day when it was more convenient. Makes sense, doesn't it? So we got as much light as possible when Charlie invited us to duke it out in the dark of night.

I guess you could say that we needed light in the darkness of night in the jungles of Viet Nam because otherwise we couldn't see where we were going or what we were doing. Regardless of the source of that light, whether helicopter light ships, flares, flashlights, cooking fires, generator-powered light bulbs (in the CP track), a full moon, or whatever, without any light we were almost helpless and couldn't tell which way to go. And that leads me to a completely different point, which is much more important than having light in the jungle even in a combat situation in the darkest night. That is having light so we can see to make our way through life itself. If this seems to be taking a bizarre turn, stick with me. It isn't bizarre at all. It isn't even strange, if you think about it. Actually, needing light to get through this life is perfectly normal and not at all hard to understand. I don't think, personally, that it's so hard to accept either. Do you agree?

This is where I turn to the basics of life. I turn to the words of Jesus Christ. He had considerable to say on this subject of light for life and living. Actually, he was a very practical man what with being Deity and all. Being the Son of God, he is in a perfect position to know what he was talking about. After all, if the Son of God doesn't know what he's talking about, then it's all over. Fortunately for us, and everyone else too, Jesus did know what he was talking about. What he said was this, "I am the light of the world. Whoever follows me will never walk in darkness, but will have the light of life." That comes from the Holy Bible book of John 8:12. The whole book of John has a lot to say about Jesus being the light of the world, how to make it through life knowing what it's all about, and where we are going when this life is over. Many folks just grope through life like a trooper groping around a fire base in the middle of a moonless night without any light to get a bearing from. With Jesus Christ to light the way, all of life comes clear. What it's all about shows up like daylight. Get it? You might want to check it out. If you want to know how to fix an M48 or an M16 you check what the manufacturer has to say in the manual. If you want to know how to fix a life and get light, you check what the Creator has to say. It's in his manual (Holy Bible). Clear? Clear as day.

19

eating dirt

DID YOU EVER EAT DIRT? YOU CRAZY, MAN? WHAT DO you mean, eat dirt? Nobody eats dirt. Why would you want to eat dirt? I eat food. I've heard of eating crow, but that's only an expression that means getting humbled. I eat lots of crow. But I sure don't eat dirt, figuratively or for real. No way. But, if you rode with the Blackhorse you ate dirt. Lots of dirt. And you didn't just eat it, you wallowed in it and you covered your body with it. The only time you didn't eat dirt was if you were in the lead track. Then you broke the ground and everyone else behind you ate dirt. Know what I mean? You've never seen dirt in the air until you've followed in a line of M48 tanks or ACavs on those jungle "highways." In the Monsoon season, mud. In the dry season, dirt. I don't mean dirt on the ground where it's supposed to be. I mean in the air, in your hair, in your ears, in your food, in your clothes, in your water, in your track. Not just regular dirt. Red clay type dirt.

I remember going along QL14 out of Loc Ninh toward Bu Dop and Bo Duc. I rode the bustle rack of an M-48, about fourth or fifth in line. Everyone wore goggles, of course, to keep the dirt out of your eyes. By the way, when I say *dirt*, I mean **dirt**. Not dust. Dirt. The kind the ground is made of. Dirt is a lot thicker than dust. Dust you wipe off. Dirt you shovel off (the exaggeration is very slight). The weather was hot and steamy. So you'd sweat. Not just perspire. Sweat. Then the dirt would land on the sweat. Lot's of it. So you got dirty. You got muddy. Riding along looking for Charlie you got muddy. I mean all over any exposed skin you would have little rivers of sweat flowing down through the mud on your arms. And eat dirt? Sure did. Great source of iron, so I'm told. I'm not sure if I believe it. But if dirt is a good source of iron then we became ironmen, for sure. You had to breath, didn't you? Naturally. So when you breathed through your nose, your nose became a cave of mud. When you opened your mouth, in went the dirt. I have no idea of any flavor. Just dirt.

Remember what that dirt did during the monsoons? Ever see a trail or a field after a squadron of M48s, ACavs, self-propelled Howitzers and whatever else ran over them and did pivot steers during a monsoon rain? Mud. Yes, real mud. I don't mean the kind we made on our arms like I said above. I mean deep, red, wet, slimy *mud*. I remember, and I'm sure you do too, mud at least two feet deep. You'd jump from one rut over a pile of mud in the road, into the other rut trying to get across. And when you missed the rut, there went your leg half way to the knee into the mud pit in the road.

Think that's bad? Wait for the dry season. When it rains, it *rains*. Monsoons are real gully-washers. But when it's dry, it's dry. I mean *dry*. It wouldn't rain a drop for weeks. But the mud was still there. Only when mud dries, it isn't mud anymore. It's hard dirt. Until the tracks come along and grind it into dry, powdery dirt. The kind that flies into the air when you drive over it. That two feet of red mud becomes two feet of red powder. Try driving in that. I just hope you enjoy dirt. Actually, it wasn't all that bad. Just another part of the "adventure." You get used to it. Which we did. The major bad about the whole thing was the getting shot at. But that's another story.

I'll tell you a real gas. Remember the Chinooks? (Yeah, I know, the s… hooks). I know that you know what I mean.

Ever see what a Chinook can do to a pile of that powdered dirt? You want to see dirt fly? Just watch a Chinook land inside the perimeter. Or watch one hover so the troops on the ground can attach a sling load to the hook under its belly. Those huge blades just suck up those mounds of powdery red clay dirt and concentrate them in the air. I took a home movie once of a Chinook hovering to pick up a sling load of stuff inside our perimeter up by Bo Duc. So much dirt is flying that you can't even see anything on the ground and you can just make out the Chinook through the red-clay cloud. After a while, your tents, your clothes, your hair, and even your skin just look red. (Hard to be a racist when everybody's skin is red, Quan Loi red, clay-red). Naturally, tents were originally OD green, boots and jungle fatigues were OD, your hair was whatever it was, but not OD, and your skin was white, black, brown, etc. But no more.

We were very fortunate, though. We had those canvas bags with a strap on top and a shower head underneath. We always left cans of water out to warm up in the sun. Then we could take a nice shower in the evening. You did that by putting water in the canvas bag and hanging it over the end of the main gun tube of the tank or off a branch if that's what you had. Unless you were busy getting shot at, of course. Then the shower had to wait. The grunts always had to wait for a stream or pond or river or something to clean up. No wonder they got jungle rot so much. We got to take hot showers a lot. We needed them. Like I just got through talking about, we had a lot of dirt to get rid of. Funny how things that were supposed to be OD turned red, like Quan Loi mud. Didn't all wash off. Didn't matter. Actually, some main things that did matter were, on the positive side: mail, food, friends, God. On the negative side: getting shot at, a buddy getting hit, getting a Dear John from the girlfriend who couldn't wait for you to get home.

Anyway, eating dirt wasn't all that bad. And cleaning up was great. (Know how to tell it's Sunday? The chaplain's wearing clean fatigues). It reminds me of some verses in the Bible where it talks about getting cleaned up from a lot of dirt. Obviously, this isn't Quan Loi red that the Bible's talking about. And it's not skin. But the lesson is clear and means a whole lot to anyone who needs cleaning—like everyone, for instance. Here're the verses: "God our Savior showed us his kindness and love. He saved us, not because of the good things we did, but because of his mercy. He washed away our sins and gave us a new life through the Holy Spirit. He generously poured out the Spirit upon us because of what Jesus Christ our Savior did. He declared us not guilty because of his great kindness. And now we know that we will inherit eternal life. These things I have told you are all true." That's from Titus 3:4-8 in the New Testament (NLT). It applies to every person who accepts them and commits to them. Then you are clean, inside. It's like being clean outside of all that mud and dirt, which only works if you take the shower.

saying goodbye

SOMETIMES SAYING GOODBYE IS HARD TO DO. SOMETIMES it isn't. Like when we've spent the work day with someone and know we'll see them tomorrow, saying goodbye is routine; a friendly gesture that we mean but give little thought to. It isn't hard at all.

Sometimes when it's not so hard, we don't think much about saying goodbye because we know we'll see the person again soon, even if not right away. For example, at our Point Man outpost meetings of Viet Nam vets, we have an enjoyable, though often intense couple of hours together. We talk about our Viet Nam experience, we encourage brothers going through hard times, we rejoice in one another's victories and healing. Then, when the meeting is over we say goodbye with a hug, a handshake, and a prayer. It means a lot. It's not as easy as saying goodbye to the neighbor as we leave the house, but we are confident we'll meet again next week, so it's OK.

It gets harder when the relationships are tight and the separations are longer, like when we see our kids off to college or our parents off on their trip home to another state. At our annual reunions of the 11th ACVVC we rekindle old friendships. We have great times seeing old buddies from Viet Nam. We relive powerful experiences. At our Philadelphia reunion a few years ago, a couple of "old troopers" came up and told me with great excitement about seeing each other in the command bunker, the large room where we socialize. One had thought for over twenty years that the other was dead, killed in a fiery helicopter crash. Now, here he was, very much alive and kicking. After a time like this, it's hard to say goodbye but well worth it for the value of what happened.

Some vets need great courage and encouragement just to come to reunions. Everyone understands. Then they come and join together as we experience great joy and healing, far beyond expectations or hopes. When the weekend is over and we have to say goodbye, we know we can meet again. We can keep in contact if we want to. And maybe we will. So the goodbye isn't too hard because now "we've been there, we've done that" and we have even greater hope for the future.

Other goodbyes are very hard. When my dad died over ten years ago, I stood alone by his casket and said goodbye. It was hard. But at the same time, I knew he had lived a full and rewarding life. He was ready to go. He definitely knew the Lord. I knew, as I looked at his lifeless body, that dad wasn't just dead. His real self had gone somewhere else. I look forward to seeing him again in eternity with Jesus.

Some goodbyes are much harder. When a son or daughter is killed in childhood, it is almost impossible to bear. Like when my sister's little girl was killed when she was four years old. When a young man or young woman is killed in their prime, it is very hard. We are forced to say goodbye knowing we'll not see them again in this life. Having a buddy killed in Viet Nam, or even years later because of what happened in Viet Nam is extremely hard. During my first tour in Viet Nam at Soc Trang in the Mekong Delta, it was hard looking into the face of Russell, one of the first of my soldiers KIA. He took a round through the forehead. It was hard to say goodbye. But we had to say it: a final goodbye. It wasn't the last during that tour or the next tour with the Blackhorse. It never got easy.

Fortunately, saying goodbye isn't the end of the matter. For one thing, *we do not forget*. Those who paid the supreme sacrifice in Viet Nam gave their lives for a noble cause. I said it then and I say it now, that cause is alive and well because of them, as well as every man or woman who put on the uniform, then went and served. Each one is part of a tradition of sacrifice that gave and still gives this land, and what it stands for, its very existence. Never forget that. Remember the bumper sticker, "For those who went and fought, liberty has a flavor the protected will never know." You know.

When we come to reunions, when we go to The Wall or a traveling Wall, when we build Viet Nam vet memorials, when we fly the POW/MIA flag, when we have Memorial Days and Veterans Days, when we do all these things, we honor the names of our buddies; we perpetuate their lives and their sacrifices. So when we have to say goodbye, even a final goodbye, it isn't the end.

One of the hardest goodbyes is when one of our own leaves us through death by disease, accident, or by their own hand. It seems so unnecessary. It seems so wrong. But we still have to say goodbye. Even then, by keeping things going, by hanging together, by looking out for our families and friends, by doing our part to keep this country great, by putting it back on a high moral plane, by keeping God in his rightful place; in these ways we keep them alive in our hearts. We serve their purpose well. That's when these tough goodbyes serve a higher purpose. Then saying goodbye isn't quite so hard.

Whether it's easy or hard, whether it's temporary or permanent, whether it's happy or sad, saying good-bye is a part of life. No one ever said otherwise. Psalm 103:13-16 says, "As a father has compassion on his children, so the Lord has compassion on those who fear him; for he knows how we are formed, he remembers that we are dust. As for man, his days are like grass, he flourishes like a flower of the field; the wind blows over it and it is gone...." But this isn't the end of the story. The Psalmist goes on to say, "But from everlasting to everlasting the Lord's love is with those who fear him, and his righteousness with their children's children—with those who keep his covenant and remember to obey his precepts" (Psalm 103:17-19).

So we realize that saying goodbye is with us to stay. But even when we have to say goodbye, even when it's hard to turn loose of someone we love, even for a short while, we are assured this isn't all there is to life. However saying goodbye affects us, one thing we can count on is the love and the presence of God. We do not have to acknowledge him; we can ignore him. We can even say goodbye to him. But, so long as we live, he will never say goodbye to us. He was and is always there. Even in Viet Nam. Even into eternity.

21

remembering

WHEN I WAS A LITTLE KID I THOUGHT HIGH SCHOOL kids were *big*! Almost like giants! I remember riding by Canoga Park High School when I was still going to Tarzana Elementary. High school looked so formidable. Then I got there. That is, after a three-year interlude at John Sutter Junior High. I even remember our old high school song—not too bad considering I graduated in 1955. The gap between grammar school and senior high was only three years, all spent in junior high. To me, as a kid, that was a *long* time. A *very* long time. Know what I mean?

When I was eighteen, I thought Model T Fords were really, really old. They were made way before I was born. So were Model As, which my dad had when he was a young guy. He used to tell me how fast they were, much faster than Model Ts. Those relics were 25 or 30 years old in the days when dad and I talked about them. They were great for converting to hot rods, of course. But very old, just the same. Now I'm 66, which I don't think is old at all. Not now, anyway. My mind goes back to 1955 very clearly. That's when I was eighteen. Corvettes were the hottest things on the road. When I was 20 I had a '57 Chevy that would turn 97 in the quarter at the San Fernando drag strip. That was over 40 years ago. Not a long time to me, not from my perspective now. But to an 18 or 20-year-old today, my Chevy would be a lot older than my dad's Model A was to me when I was that age. Same goes for the '58 Corvette I had after the '57 Chevy. My Corvette was the fastest one in Van Nuys back in 1960. It seems like only yesterday. But it wasn't yesterday.

We remember other things the same way. Think about it. You're not part of the young generation anymore. You don't believe me? Check your driver's license. Check your birth certificate. Look in the mirror. Ask your teenage kid—he'll tell you. Clearly. Or, if you have an early-twenties daughter, ask her. Better yet, ask your grandkids. Just the thought of having grandkids will bring a reality check! Grandkids are great! But you don't have them at age 19 or 20. Looking back, it's easy to remember so much so clearly—like it was yesterday. Sure, some is fuzzy, but the rest is clear.

Think about your family when you were a kid. Think about your first day in school. Think about your first girl friend. Think about your first car. Think about your first kiss (didn't know you could kiss so clumsy, did you? But you learned, you just needed practice). Think about your wedding, your first baby, your first job, your first draft notice! What? Your first draft notice!? Now you're spoiling a nice dream. Or, if you weren't drafted, remember your recruiter? What about your first white-sidewall haircut, your first night in the barracks, your first lap around the parade field, your first (and only, for most) trip to Viet Nam. What? Viet Nam! Why bring up Viet Nam? Mostly because it was such an important part of your life, even if you're a family member whose boyfriend, son, or husband went to Viet Nam (or girlfriend, daughter, or wife). Bring it up again because Viet Nam is a prominent part of your life. Because Viet Nam was such a defining event in your life. It helped a whole lot in making you the man that you are today. Like someone said, "Character is formed in the crucible of adversity." I know that's a trite old saying, but trite old sayings become trite because they express so much wisdom that's worth repeating.

Actually, we really don't even want to forget Viet Nam. We don't forget school. We don't forget church. We don't forget Uncle Joe or Aunt Maggie. We don't forget Cub Scouts or Little League. We don't forget that weasel of a dog next door that bit us in the butt just because we were messing with her pups. We don't forget the best school teacher we ever had. We don't forget the events or the people that shaped our lives, especially the really powerful events and people. We don't want to forget them. And why should we? I admit we sometimes have to adjust to the hard parts. But that doesn't mean we should forget the rest.

Let's be a little more specific about Viet Nam. We'd have a hard time coming up with an experience more powerful for us than living through a tour in Viet Nam (or any other war). Viet Nam is decades behind us now. We've grown and changed. A lot has happened since then. Memories might seem like yesterday, but they weren't yesterday. They were a long time ago. But we don't forget. And when it comes to our buddies, we don't want to forget. For the buddy we shared the dangers of combat with, we don't forget. For those we shared C rations or monsoon rains with, we don't forget. For those wounded in body or mind and spirit, we don't forget. We may be years apart in time since we were together and we may live miles apart now. But we don't forget. We honor each other. We come together when we can. Together we remember, and in a small way we relive and rejoice.

Our greatest honor is given to our buddies who didn't come home. They are our greatest heroes. We love them. We remember them. We live to make sure their sacrifice counted. Whatever other people may think is their business. For us, we honor those who answered their country's call when they were needed and paid with their lives. We honor their families. We honor and remember our POW/MIAs. We will not forget. We will always remember. Those men are our brothers. Those men are our heroes.

Through all this *we remember God Almighty*, maker of Heaven and Earth. He was there. He brought us through. Sometimes we felt him, sometimes we didn't. But he was there all the time. Some of us, his choice young ones, he took to be with himself. God also took to himself his own divine son, Jesus Christ, at a young age. The Roman soldiers killed him by crucifixion at age 33. He was killed so whoever wants to believe could be free *forever*, more than just here and now. After that he rose from the dead on the third day (Easter) proving that killing the body is not the end of everything. He made the way to heaven. That's the "end" of everything, and heaven is *forever*.

One of history's greatest warriors, King David, wrote the Twenty-Third Psalm in the Bible. I thought maybe you'd like to read it. It fits what we're talking about:

"The Lord is my shepherd, I shall not be in want. He makes me lie down in green pastures, he leads me beside quiet waters, he restores my soul. He guides me in the paths of righteousness for his name's sake. Even though I walk through the valley of the shadow of death, I will fear no evil, for you are with me; your rod and staff, they comfort me. You prepare a table for me in the presence of my enemies. You anoint my head with oil; my cup overflows. Surely goodness and mercy will follow me all the days of my life, and I will dwell in the house of the Lord forever" (Psalm 23 NIV).

God bless our heroes. God bless our buddies. God bless our families. God bless the USA.

22

home

WHEN YOU WERE A LITTLE KID OUT PLAYING WITH YOUR friends and things didn't go right, what did you do about it? If you were like me or most other little kids, you shouted at your friends, "I'm going home!" And you took your ball and you went home! In your heart you knew you'd be back later. It always worked that way. Kids are like that. You had your friends to play with and go to school with. When someone hurt you or things didn't go well, you cried or just got mad, took your ball, and went home to mom. You knew that's where you belonged and where your world would come back together so you could go play again tomorrow. You got a Band-Aid for your knee and a hug for your feelings.

What about now? Where is home for you now? For five years I lived in Darien, just outside Chicago. I even owned a house—me and the bank, that is. I had a job too. When I would leave my office after a hard day's work, I would go home. I could relax, lean back, and cool it. I mowed the grass and fixed the car. My wife would come home, turn on the tube, get dinner, then we ate it. Then she would go to her hobbies. We did what you do when you're at home. But you know what? When I think of *home* home, when I think of where I really *belong*, it isn't in Darien where I lived. I liked it where I lived. It was a wonderful neighborhood. My neighbors were terrific, friendly people. I loved them. But my house wasn't *home*. Home is Southern California. Where the fruits and nuts hang out. I'll admit that maybe I'm one of the original nuts. However, I'm not one of the fruits. Nope. Home is where I grew up. Home is where my roots are. Home is where I go when I go home to see family. Home is where I still have my church membership. Home is where I went dove hunting in the desert with my friends. They're still my friends even though our hunting grounds are long gone to the developers. Home is where I *feel* like I belong even though I'll probably never live there again. I realize you can never go back to how things used to be. Everything changes. Nothing goes backward. But I can still *feel* that way about *home*. And I do.

Remember Viet Nam? (What a question!) We used to think about *home* all the time. Whether we came from a rich home or a poor home, whether home was a farm or a tract house, whether our home was peaceful and serene or tumultuous and busy, it was where we knew our place and were comfortable in our own way. Over in Viet Nam we thought about *home* a lot. In the jungles or in the rice paddies, we were home with our buddies and our gear. It was where we belonged at the time. We looked out for each other; we shared a personal and powerful experience together. We got tight with each other. We lived a raw, primitive, and dangerous lifestyle, but we did it together. We were brothers. We still are. It was home, even if it wasn't *home*. You know very well what I mean.

Some of us lived in tents out there in the jungle along the Cambodian border. I did. I was the chaplain so I had a tent. My assistant and I had a GP small tent (full of holes, but still a tent). We had cots. We slept rolled up in poncho liners. We had artillery ammo pallets for a floor. We even had a shower bucket hung outside from a tree limb or something to shower (hot in the evening from being in the sun all day). That was home even as I dreamed of *home*. I used to spend a lot of time with the recon troops, including at night (many stories about that). I was sort of an honored guest. That meant they loaned me a cot and a poncho. I sometimes slept in the CP tent on the cot. I remember, though, one night when I got a cot and poncho, but there wasn't a CP tent to sleep in. The cot was next to the ACav of my hosts for the night. We stretched the poncho from the ACav to the ground. The cot was underneath the poncho for protection. It rained. I mean it *rained*. It was the monsoon season and it rained! I know you remember what I'm talking about. I had the choice of getting my head rained on all night or my feet. So my feet got rained on all night. As you know, cots tend to sag in the middle. So while my head was out of the rain and my feet were getting rained on, my middle was lying in a puddle of water. Such was life in the jungle with the Blackhorse along the Cambodian border. But that was home. Sound weird? OK. Still, if you were there, it was home for you too and you know what I mean. And a lot of you didn't have a cot. It wasn't *home*, but it was home. It was where our buddies were, our brothers. It was where we found shelter, food, camaraderie. It was where we were really needed. Strange, wasn't it? Yes. But very real. Very powerful. Very memorable. Home.

When I think of home I think of many things, even to this day. But home means a lot more than the past or where I feel the best. When I think of home I also think of the future. I don't mean just the future when I retire for good. I don't mean just when life slows down and I can spend all the time I want fishing, playing golf, at which I'm a wannabe, or having fun with the grandkids. I think of *home* after I'm gone from this life. For, after all is said and done, this life is really only the preparation for the next life, which is even more real. Home *forever* counts *forever*. An old gospel song I loved as a kid went something like this: "This world is not my home; I'm just a-passing through. My treasures are laid up somewhere beyond the blue. I know he'll take me through, though I am weak and poor, and I can't feel at home in this world any more." That's what life is all about, when all is said and done. And you can count on it; it will soon enough be all said and done.

Jesus said in the Bible, "Do not let your hearts be troubled. Trust in God; trust also in me. In my Father's house are many rooms; if it were not so, I would have told you. I am going there to prepare a place for you. And if I go and prepare a place for you, I will come back and take you to be with me that you also may be where I am" (John 14:1-3).

That's what home is really all about. Call it heaven. Call it forever. Call it for certain. The fact is that someday, I'm going *home*. And when I get *home* that's where I'll stay. Forever.

23

coming home

One day last January I was browsing the book section in a PX (I retired after 27 years as an active duty Army chaplain so can still use the PX). I came across a paperback called *Homecoming* by Bob Greene (Ballantine Books, New York, 1989). He had heard stories for years about Vietnam veterans who, upon returning home, were spat on as they arrived in the USA. He was incredulous that such an occurrence could be true, even during the days of riots and conflicts of the late sixties and early seventies. He decided to find out for himself. "I raised the question in my syndicated newspaper column…. More than two million Vietnam veterans came back alive. It is to those veterans that I posed the question (page 2): 'Were you spat upon when you returned from Vietnam?'"

The response to Greene's question was astonishing. He received replies from over a thousand veterans with virtually all telling their story. Many were actually spat upon; and not just by hippy-weirdoes, either. Some were spat upon by "little old ladies" and other "normal" people. Of course, many were not spat upon at all. Of these, many did not really believe it ever happened. Then, of the hundreds of respondents, many told of a different story of their "welcome home," some worse than being spat upon.

For example, among the replies of those who were spat upon (from page 15), "I was medically evacuated from Vietnam in November, 1969 to a Naval hospital in Japan where, after my recovery, I was stationed…. In early 1970 I was transferred back to the USA. My family and I landed at San Francisco International Airport after a very long flight from Japan. We were going into the cafeteria to eat and, of course, I was in my uniform with all my Vietnam medals, including the Purple Heart and the Gold Star. My family and I were standing in line, when out of the blue, this middle-aged lady walked up to me with a bowl of potato salad in her hand. She threw the salad in the middle of my chest and spat what she had in her mouth in my face. Then she proceeded to call me a 'baby killer,' 'war monger' and a lot of other vile names."

Of those not spat upon, their stories are varied. Perhaps, typical is on page 85; "As a five-tour combat veteran, I have never been spat upon nor have I ever known of a Vietnam veteran so treated. As I recall, their most frustrating treatment, at the hands of a minority of the public, was indifference."

Other incidents did occur that could be seen as worse than being spit on. For instance, on pages 177-8; "I received a gunshot wound in Vietnam in September 1968, and on my return home in late October I was required to change planes and airlines at Chicago's O'Hare Airport. I was on crutches and wearing a full leg cast. I was also trying to carry a travel bag, which was rather difficult, as I was inexperienced on crutches. A pair of college-age males walked up on either side of me and one of them asked if I was returning from Vietnam. I replied that I was, and they asked a couple more questions about my injury and acted very friendly. Suddenly they kicked my crutches out from under me, pointed and laughed at me on the floor, then took off running…. Although I remember this experience very vividly, what I remember more is the concern and help that I received from other people who witnessed the incident."

These stories are poignant and powerful. Each of us has his or her own story to tell of homecoming (don't forget, many were women; nurses, donut dollies and other female soldiers, etc.). We all are acutely aware that there were no bands, no parades, and such as in other wars of this country. However it happened, each of our "homecomings" was the sort of experience we do not forget.

Why am I writing in such detail about such stories from the past? Why am I resurrecting old history that many think should be long forgotten? Because these stories are powerful. Because we each have our own stories that have such a strong influence on our lives, even today. Because so many of us have not resolved these matters properly. Because some of us are still living these events as if they were only yesterday. Because they were not yesterday; they were many years ago and it is time we treat them as history and not as present reality. Powerful as our experiences were, they are history. We must never forget our history, but we must be wise and discerning in how we relate to that personal history (same for our nation, but that's another subject).

It's time to put our Vietnam experiences in perspective. Many vets, of course, have already done so. Some are in the process. Some of you need to get started. Healing, forgiveness, sharing, learning from experiences, teaching others, including our sons and daughters, reconciling with those we may have hurt or who may have hurt us; these all go together toward making the vet a whole, mature, strong man. The Bible talks about our character being refined by fire in a similar way as gold is refined by fire. The Vietnam vet (and his family members who shared with him or her) has the extraordinary opportunity to take the power of his experiences and use them to gain insight, understanding, patriotism, compassion, and values. He can grow in ways the person who was not there can never understand.

To close, I would like to quote Jesus in the parable of the talents (Matthew 25:21). Speaking of great "Welcome

Homes," God wants to welcome you now and at your accounting day, in the words of Jesus: "Well done, good and faithful servant! You have been faithful with a few things; I will put you in charge of many things. Come and share you Master's happiness!"

This will, indeed, be a worthy homecoming. I will hear the words, "Welcome Home," as I enter the gates of heaven. You can too. Will you?

24

it don't mean nuthin'

REMEMBER THE PHRASE, "IT DON'T MEAN NUTHIN'"? I don't think it's used much any more. But in Viet Nam it was used *a lot*. It was a funny sort of phrase. I don't know what you call it when someone says something exactly opposite to what he means, but this phrase proves the point. You could be sure that when a young soldier said, "It don't mean nuthin," that something had happened that meant *plenty*. It was something that had to be pushed down, repressed, and denied in order to cope in the context of where he was and what was going on at the time.

So many were so young. The average age of the Viet Nam soldier, as you probably know, was 19. That means there were a lot of 17-year-olds to balance off us 30-year-olds to average out to 19. Just being "in country" with all that was happening was stressful enough. Going virtually alone into a new and strange culture, climate, and war was a shock in itself. Not knowing who the enemy was was a stressor. Maybe the little kid begging candy had a grenade strapped to his back. Maybe your last patrol was a bummer. Maybe the old man's driver was a VC. So in the middle of all this, you get a Dear John from your fiancé along with the diamond ring you gave her taped to the letter. Out in the jungle, your best buddy, your brother in arms, steps on a mine and blows his leg off.

You carry him to the LZ for the medevac helicopter to pick him up (or his body). You don't even know his last name, only his handle, his nickname (Snake, Wild Man, Deacon, or John). You worked like a dog getting your M48 tank or your ACav ready for action and it takes an RPG, completely demolishing it. How do you handle the stress, the traumatic event, so you can survive the next firefight, the next unfair assignment—walking point when it's not your turn? You jam it deep inside: "It don't mean nuthin'." You know exactly what I'm talking about. You said it too. Maybe many times.

That's fine. The phrase served a very useful purpose. The Viet Nam soldiers were young and needed to cope. Besides, when you said the event didn't mean *anything*, your buddies all knew it meant *everything*. The communication was clear. It also meant "end of subject." It meant you couldn't handle it then and there and that you were postponing dealing with it. Everyone knew that and left you alone because it was the same for them. It hurt too bad, went too deep, or meant too much, and you couldn't handle it at the time. So you pushed it down and everyone respected your space and you respected theirs.

Viet Nam vets understand these things. Whether conscious or not, it's a gut matter. It's one reason why many Viet Nam vets think, rightly or wrongly, that only another Viet Nam vet can understand where they're coming from. I expect this all applies to vets of other wars equally.

Now, it's time; indeed, it's way late, for every Viet Nam vet to deal with these repressed, pushed down matters and get them resolved. *It can be done.* For many, these "don't mean nuthin'" matters are resolved and are pure history. Unfortunately, for way too many, they are still not resolved and are causing too much disruption in present living. There is a way out. The light at the end of the tunnel is the light at the end of the tunnel and is *not* the headlight of an oncoming freight train!

Bruce and Wayne, my friends, you did not have to take your own lives this year. I am so sorry you did not see the way out. I grieve for you with your families and with so many who wanted to help, who could have understood and seen you through this. God rest your souls. I will not say, "It don't mean nuthin'" because it means so much. It still hurts deeply that you are gone and we, your brothers, your families, those who were close, could not help enough to get you through the bad times these many years later.

For all of us, brothers and sisters in arms, families and loved ones, may we never again say, "It don't mean nuthin." Those days are past. Let us all keep on reaching out to each other in healing and forgiveness, helping, supporting, accepting help, opening up, and loving. We know, in fact, that all that happened really did mean something. It still does. It means a lot.

I need to close this off for now, even though there is so much more to be said. Let me just quote from the words of Jesus the Christ, because he is the living Word of God to us. He knows whereof he speaks:

"Come to me all you who are weary and burdened, and I will give you rest. Take my yoke upon you and learn from me for I am gentle and humble in heart, and you will find rest for your souls. For my yoke is easy and my burden is light" (Holy Bible, Matthew 11:28-30, NIV).

25

opening old wounds

REGARDING "IT DON'T MEAN NUTHIN'," YOU KNOW ALL about it, don't you? It was about when something real hard or traumatic happened and you couldn't deal with it right then because you were too busy shooting or too busy just surviving. Maybe a buddy was hit right beside you and you couldn't save him. Maybe you had to do something extremely hard or very ugly, like shoot at someone up close. You learned why they say war is hell. Whatever happened, you had to stuff it to keep from going crazy so you could keep functioning as a soldier in your squad or wherever you were. After all, the other guys were depending on you like you were depending on them. Know what I mean? Real well. You were there.

Every once in a while, even now, I'm reminded about stuffing it. I still hear from families and close friends of vets who say their man just won't talk about Viet Nam (or Korea, Desert Storm, or WWII). "He clams up when I ask." "I'm afraid to ask." "I think he's going off the deep end." You know a vet like that? Are you one? Could be. I agree there's no need to keep blabbing about it all the time. OK. But sometimes there is a need to talk, to open up, to just stop jamming it in and going it alone—even at the risk of opening up old wounds. Actually, that's how a lot of wounds get healed.

Open them up. Expose them to the air. Let it out. Like I said, every once in a while I'm reminded of that old need to stuff it. But that was back in the Nam. Then was then. Now is now. Now I hear from women or kids or even other vets who have a man, a dad, a friend who still has it stuffed after all these years. Trouble is, now it comes out, leaks out, or explodes out in ways that even the "stuffer" doesn't mean, didn't intend. Thirty-some years later, it's still stuffed. And it shouldn't be. It's time…no, it's past time, to unstuff. Why, to this day there are vets living in the woods that are still fighting that war. They're living like hermits, surrounded by trip wires and automatic ambushes. Some are drinking themselves into oblivion ("I'm not alcoholic." "I can handle it." Yeah, sure). Some are self-medicating on drugs. Or they're mad at the world. Or they're just plain mad all the time and don't even know why.

On the other hand, plenty of vets unstuffed long ago. I remember one of the first nights after we finally went into Cambodia. Our How Battery stayed on the Viet Nam side to fire support for the recon troops who crossed the border. Some of our cannon cockers were sleeping in a tent when a 107mm rocket landed just outside, slid into the tent, and went off between two of the troopers. Both of them lost a leg, one his right and the other his left, each just below the knee. I don't need to describe the misery or the trauma. You know that subject well enough already. I heard what happened when they were on the way to the aid station at Quan Loi so I got over there when they were brought in. They were stabilized and sent on to the rear to the evac hospital. Some years later I was stationed in the same state as one of them so I went to visit him. I'll call him Jim, which is not his name. Jim was doing very well. He had a nice family, a good job, a nice home, and he said all was fine. He could, and did, talk about his Viet Nam experience, his healing, and how it all fit into his life now. Which was just fine. Looked to me like everything that might have been stuffed at one time was unstuffed now. It wasn't hard to see. Goes to show it can be done.

Another story: When I was stationed in Northern Virginia I went down to The Wall on Memorial Day and Veterans Day and talked to the guys. I was in uniform and when vets would spot the Blackhorse patch they would open up and talk. They could see that I was a chaplain and maybe that helped. I guess with some it didn't. Mostly Viet Nam vets at The Wall liked to talk. About a lot of things. It was very healing. It was, and is, a very good and safe place to let old wounds open up, hit the air, and start the healing. It was, and is, a very good place to get "unstuffed." I remember one vet in particular. He was in a wheelchair. I don't remember his name. He was with his wife, his son, and a Viet Nam vet buddy. He belonged to a Viet Nam vets group down in Texas. The guys there had taken up a collection and then his buddy got in his old, decrepit van and drove him with his wife and son to The Wall. He wanted to look up the name of his closest friend on The Wall so he could say goodbye before he died. He had only six months to live from whatever it was that put him into the wheelchair. With his wife, his son, and his friend, he did just that. He said goodbye to his closest friend in Viet Nam. I was so happy that his buddy's name on The Wall was near the bottom where he could easily see it. Before he died, he was able to unstuff himself and get a whole lot of healing. A good way to finish off.

A point of this story is that I believe every Viet Nam soldier (or Marine, sailor, airman or civilian support person) had a lot of stress (or should I say trauma?) to deal with. Many stuffed it, maybe most did. Some didn't. It was stuffed because it was just too much to handle at that time and place, especially for those out in the bush where most of the most traumatic things happened. But in the rear too. The rear wasn't always a cakewalk. You know what I mean. I don't have to be graphic to make the point. Some were able to deal with it, to not stuff it, right away. Some took longer. Some a lot longer. And some haven't unstuffed it yet. Regardless of which category you fit in, don't ever forget, we're all brothers and we're all in this together. For the few who didn't then or don't now consider themselves part of the brotherhood, OK. And when I say brothers, I mean sisters included, because we all know the greatness of the nurses, the donut dollies, and all the other women who were there and were part of the "brotherhood." So, for you who are still stuffing it, come on out. It isn't worth it to keep stuffing and it isn't necessary. For you who have unstuffed, remember your brothers who haven't and help them out. Show them the way. For you who never had to stuff anything at all, and there aren't too many of you, share your strength. Be open and available. We all need each other. Even these decades and years later. Let me add one more thing, this is not a matter of rank. Clear? 'Nuf said? Comprende?

Finally, I would like to quote from the most reliable and powerful source for help and healing. It is the place that tells the way to really unstuff and to become healed, whole and put together right. If you know me at all, you'll know I'm talking about the Holy Bible, the Word of God. Now if you're fading out, starting to examine the inside of your eyelids or going into a thousand-yard stare, hang in for a minute longer. Realize that now is the time for grasping the meaning of what this is all about. Here is a realistic and reliable word of advice: "Give all your worries and cares to God, for he cares about what happens to you. Be careful! Watch out for attacks from the Devil, your great enemy. He prowls around like a roaring lion, looking for some victim to devour. Take a firm stand against him, and be strong in your faith. Remember that Christians all over the world are going through the same kind of suffering you are. In his kindness God called you to his eternal glory by means of

Jesus Christ. After you have suffered a little while, he will restore, support, and strengthen you, and he will place you on a firm foundation" (1 Peter 5:7-10, New Living Translation of the Holy Bible).

A *lot* of vets have come out of the biggest cases of stuffing through this word of advice. You can too. OK? OK. Allons!

26

thank a vet

"IF YOU LOVE YOUR FREEDOM, THANK A VET!" HOW MANY times have you seen that bumper sticker? It's one of my favorites, and I've seen a lot of bumper stickers. It's catchy and has a touch of wit about it, even though it's not funny. It delivers a strong and important truth some of us believe Americans need to think about. It's a statement from the heart of anyone who understands where our liberties and freedoms come from. The message is that a price has been paid for the rights we all enjoy. Those rights, those freedoms, those liberties didn't just come out of thin air. King George of England sure didn't give them to us. No one just gave them to us. They were bought with a price, which the veteran paid, and the price was high.

"Freedom isn't free." I don't know who said it first, but he knew what he was talking about. This is a wonderful world because God made it that way. Just the same, there's a lot of "slime" out there. Life can be beautiful but life can be brutal. There's always someone who wants to take other people's freedoms, then destroy or control them. There's always someone out there who just wants the power, wealth, or whatever, and they'll stomp on anyone or overrun any place to get it. This happens between people and it happens between countries. When it happens on a personal level, someone has to stop the bad guy. When it happens on a national level, someone still has to stop it. That's the man in the uniform. It's the soldier who does the work. It's the veteran who has done it.

There is always a Hitler, a Hussein or someone who would be glad to take your freedom and grind you under so he can "have it all." That's just how it is. There is always someone who will cut you a deal and then run his tanks and weapons of mass destruction across your land and through your people. All you have to do is look the other way. Vets didn't look the other way.

Whenever the need has arisen in America, there have been men and women who answered the call, who wore the uniform, who did what had to be done, from the American Revolution to Iraqi Freedom, including Viet Nam. Whatever the politicians and spinmasters have to say, the fact is that the Viet Nam vet, just as every vet, responded to the need, put on the uniform, put his/her life on the line and kept the people of this country free. We are so free that we have even elected leaders that never wore that uniform and understand little of this country's military heritage and indebtedness to its veterans. And that's OK because it shows without doubt that we are still free to vote our own mind. Our vets have seen to it.

Let's talk about another kind of freedom. This goes beyond our American freedoms which we have been discussing. Many vets, including Viet Nam vets, have fought and died for our country's freedoms. Most of these men and women have proceeded to the point in their lives where Viet Nam is behind them, they have adjusted well, and they are getting on with their lives. There are others, though, who are not experiencing the personal freedom they need because they are still tied to their Viet Nam experience. Some avoid thinking about the whole thing at all. Some can't visit The Wall. Not because they don't have opportunity, but because they can't bring themselves to go. It would open the shadowy corners of their minds and renew memories they can't handle.

That is not freedom. For you who are still tied to your past and lacking freedom to deal with it, I assure you that you are not alone. There are plenty of brothers and sisters from other wars that are tied to their past the same as you. That means WWII, Korea, Granada, Desert Storm, Panama, or others. It also means other situations like terrorist bombings, airplane crashes, and victims of rape. Make your own application. I urge all of you to go to someone who can help you break loose from your bondage to your past. Help is there.

There is a third freedom you need to think about. You need this freedom as much as our nation needs its liberties and the vet needs his freedom from bondage to his past. I'm talking about spiritual freedom. Whoa now, don't stop reading here. Keep cool. I've been down this road and so have plenty of other vets. This road to freedom goes where you need to be—free from being what you don't want to be. Jesus told his disciples in John 8:32, "…you will know the truth and the truth will set you free." This could get real deep. For now, I just want to point out that everyone who was ever born is subject to what I call the human predicament. Think about it: do you *always* do what you want to do or behave how you really want to behave (always)? Do you *always* do the right thing? Do you *always* say the right words? Do you *ever* hurt a loved one because you have a mean streak and you really want to hurt them? Do you know *anyone* who is perfect? Do you know *anyone* who has never lied, cheated, stolen, or done anything wrong? Including you? Our predicament is that we are not perfectly what we ought to be and it causes problems for us all. Put it all together and you can see how it causes problems for the whole world.

When Jesus said you shall know the truth, part of what he was talking about was this human predicament. Everyone is part of it. It's what causes wars, fights, disease, accidents, and everything else that's wrong with this world. We're tied to it. When Jesus said we could be set free of it he meant that we could enjoy freedom from this predicament. He paid the price for this freedom. The price was high. Veterans understand that. Many people don't appreciate the price paid for their spiritual freedom. Often they don't comprehend where that freedom comes from. Many don't even recognize their need for freedom because they don't see how bound they really are. Sound familiar?

This human predicament is what God calls sin. It's what ties us and keeps us from the freedom of being what we we're created for. It's not hard to understand. In some ways, it's like the PTSD vet who isn't yet set free from his past and may not even recognize his problem. American's freedoms are there for the taking. For vets, freedom from memories of war experiences and traumas are there for the taking too. So is freedom from our human predicament, from sin. I hope you will take advantage of all these kinds of freedom. They can be yours. They can be yours now.

For your American freedoms, *Thank a Vet!*
For your spiritual freedom, *Thank the Lord!*

27

changing

HOW MANY TIMES HAVE YOU HEARD IT SAID THAT THE only sure things in life are death and taxes? There's some truth to that and there's a little humor too. But it's definitely not everything that's sure in life. I can think of lots more. So can you. For instance, a part of life that's true for everyone is change. Just plain old change, as in becoming different. You know, one day you have lots of hair, next day you're bald or one day you're young and skinny, next time you check, you're middle aged and not so skinny. Things like that. Change can come in large or small doses. It may come on strong or it may come on weak. You may like it or you may not. But this I know, change happens to everyone, including you and me. If you're moving, breathing and thinking, you're changing.

Think about it. Remember the day you stepped off the airplane into the stifling heat and humidity of Viet Nam? Remember the uncertainty, the anxiety, the apprehension, the fear of the unknown, later to become the fear of the known? You changed forever. Some would say you grew up—call it what you want, but you sure changed. Remember the day you were married? Remember your first child (those of you with kids)? Remember your first car? Remember your first run-in with the law (hopefully, just a traffic ticket, but who knows). What about the time you offered to go out on

129

patrol in your buddy's place so he could have some rest? What about the times you did something hard so a friend could have a break—or to save his life? You've followed through on decisions about work, where to vacation, where to live, whether to stay in the Army (whaaat?). All of the above affected your life, proving that you are changing, constantly changing. If you're breathing, you're changing. Hopefully, changing for the better. Hopefully, changing means you're growing, becoming more mature—even if you're 80, or hoping to be 80 someday. One thing for sure, you're a day older than you were yesterday and you're a day closer to 80 than you were yesterday. That's change.

I'm 66. So what's that got to do with anything, you say? So #1: I was never sure I'd make it this far, if you know what I mean. #2: I was retired from the Army for four years and then went back to work. You say, "Are you nuts?" (Probably, what with being from California.) Was that such a big deal? Yes, it was such a big deal. I was having a good time living in a fifth-wheel trailer with my wife and traveling all over the country. We were visiting family, friends, living where we wanted, moving when we felt like it, and doing chaplain things with vets, mostly Viet Nam vets. Then, through a lot of circumstances over eight or nine months, a clear call of God came to accept a "cool" position in a suburb of Chicago. So I went back to work as chaplain for a retirement community serving about 650 seniors and developing programs in many other places. (Our resident's average age was 83. When I complained about being old at 64, they replied, "Sonny, you don't know what old is.") I want you to know that I learned a whole lot at this stage of my life. I grew and changed plenty. What's this got to do with you? Well, I figure that if I can make such important changes at this time of my life then you can too. I'm not so different from you or anyone else. Like I said, if you're breathing, you're changing.

Now, I say again, so what? So, since you're changing, it only makes sense, considering that you're not a brick, that you use your God-given ability to decide for yourself *how* you're going to change. There are more excuses for not changing than Ho Chi Minh has sandals. You probably use a lot of those excuses for yourself. You may even have some originals. There are plenty of old, worn out ones like, "I'm too young," "I'm too old," "I'm too tired," "I'm too busy," "I'm too far gone," "I'm too hopeless," "I'm too thick in the head" (which may be true!), "I'm too good already" (I doubt that), or even "I just don't want to change." None of these are original. They are common as grass, the kind you walk on and mow. I admit that last excuse is blatantly honest. But, whether you *want* to change or not doesn't determine *whether* you'll change. It only determines *how* you'll change.

So, let's get on with it. Decide what your goals are. Clarify your values. Accept what you know is best. Keep your eyes on your "higher power" as AA would say or, best yet, on your "*Highest* Power," Almighty God, as the Word of God would say. Set your goals high. Seek healing from the more traumatic experiences and changes that happened in your life like Viet Nam, national indifference to Nam vets, divorce, injury, betrayal, abuse. Many "challenges" become barriers in our lives that cause us to stumble and sometimes fall. But, get up or, better yet, let God pick you up. Get on with life. After all, change can be for the spectacularly good. Even the Viet Nam experience wasn't all bad, which I've written about somewhere else. Anyone who's come to reunions knows firsthand that many good things came out of those days. The camaraderie, the good times, the fun memories, these things prove my point. Margaret the dog and Charlie the chicken are worth remembering. These things changed our lives. Maybe the change was small, but a lot of small changes make a big change. Right? Right. Anyway, you get the point.

My final point is that the biggest, the best, the eternally rewarding change you can make for your life is to put yourself in the hand of the One who made you and created a great plan for your life. Why else would we still be here, after all we've been through? There is a reason for you and your life. One of my favorite sections of the Bible is King Solomon's words in Proverbs 3:5-6: "Trust in the Lord with all your heart and lean not on your own understanding. In all your ways acknowledge him and he shall direct your paths" (NKJV). That's why I went back to work. And, after working for five years, I went back into retirement and on the road again. We're back to living in a motor home. This time I have a cell phone and e-mail. Before, we had to rely on pay phones and snail mail. Sure is easier to keep in touch now. Sure is a wonderful change in my lifestyle. See what I mean about change?

So you see change is part of life. Whether it's beneficial or detrimental is up to you. Whether it's growing in ways you decide or whether life is just what happens is entirely up to you. Actually, when you think about it, life with its growth and change is pretty exciting and can be a wonderful adventure. I sincerely hope it is for you.

28

where was god

ONE OF THE MOST PROFOUND QUESTIONS I HAVE encountered coming out of the Vietnam War experience is, "Where was God in Vietnam?" I served two tours in country: The first was in the Mekong Delta when we went through the Tet Offensive of 1968, and the second was with the 11th Armored Cavalry Regiment, the Blackhorse, when we went into Cambodia. I have experienced and witnessed combat and its horrors. I am sensible enough, however, to recognize that my own experience pales into insignificance compared to what many others went through. I can still say with confidence, from being there and from the word of many witnesses and combatants, that God was right there all the time.

While I knew, felt, and observed God's presence in trying and difficult situations, I well understand why so many honestly ask the question, "Where was God?" and they honestly say that they did not feel him there. So many experiences were so horrible, traumatic, and unspeakable that many men and women honestly believe that God had abandoned them. I could relate many of the stories. You can too. Some of the stories could be your own of how you accidentally killed someone you are convinced was innocent (a child, perhaps), stories of watching your buddies die horribly and violently, stories of abject fear or excruciating suffering and mutilation, stories of trying so hard to save a life, only to have it slip away, stories of terrible guilt because others died when you think it should have been you.

I am so sorry you had to live through those experiences. War is indeed hell. Perhaps we can talk someday about "Why does God let evil happen?" But, about "Where was God in Vietnam?" I assure you, with the full authority of God's Word, my own experiences, and those of many, many others, that God was right there all the time. He never left you. He never abandoned you. There are many things I cannot understand, but one thing I do understand is that God would never, and did not ever, abandon you, even under the most trying of times. I cannot say the opposite is true. Maybe you did abandon God. I know that I, even as a chaplain, often neglected or compromised my relationship with God. But he is reliable whereas I am only human.

In the Bible, the New Testament book of Hebrews 13:5 quotes the Old Testament book of Deuteronomy 31:6 where God says, "The Lord your God goes with you; he will never leave you or forsake you." King David in Psalm 23 says, "Even though I walk through the valley of the shadow of death, I will fear no evil, for you are with me." These people were in a position to know what they were talking about. The Israelites under Moses entered the Promised Land of Israel in a military operation. King David was one of the greatest military leaders of his day. He had been there in the thick of battle many times. He shed much blood. He did not evade the draft or run from danger. When these people recognized God was with them, they knew it was true. They still had to face the realities and the traumas that are often a part of life, especially in war. But they did it knowing God was there. This truth brought them through. It wasn't just a matter of military victory. It was a matter of spiritual health and total well-being.

I want you to know, whoever you are and whatever your experience, that in Viet Nam, through the years since, and right now, God is there. Whether you were a tunnel rat, a grunt, an ACAV driver, helicopter door gunner, medic, cook, pencil-pusher, clerk, nurse, chaplain, commander, or whatever, God has not, is not, and will never abandon you. NEVER. I hope you will open yourself to him, because you do have it in your power to abandon him. Jesus said in Revelation 3:20, "Here I am. I stand at the door and knock. If anyone hears my voice and opens the door, I will come in to him and eat with him, and he with me."

You may notice that this chapter is rather short, simple, and to the point. I have not tried to prove what I say. God's presence in Viet Nam is the same as his presence in your life today. He's there all the time, but won't force himself on you or anyone else. Viet Nam, like all war, is a particularly hard and nasty situation for anyone caught in the fire. This is true. No one that I know of ever said war wasn't hell on earth. So, for some, I'm sure it is especially hard to see God there. I expect this is where a person needs to be particularly open to God's presence. This is a reason I used King David as an example from the Bible of a warrior who served on the edge and in the crosshairs. He knew God was there all the time. One thing I especially appreciate about the Bible is that it doesn't dodge the issues, it doesn't try to soft pedal the Word of God, and it's very open about the seamy side of life. It recognizes the problems people bring upon themselves and the world, even upon the innocent. The Bible even talks about King David's sins, including adultery and murder. But God's Word also recognizes that there are answers. One of the answers is the reliable presence of God.

One of the best answers coming out of the Viet Nam war is that, regardless of the mess so many brought to bear, *God Was There All the Time.*

29

a driving force

THE FORCE THAT DRIVES WHAT WE ALL ARE AND WHAT we do is power, plain power. Power is what makes it possible to do what we want and to be what we want. It's also what makes it possible for us to make other people do what we want—or for other people to make us do what they want. It's like a flashlight or the Energizer bunny, with the power of the battery it can run, without the force of the battery power, it can't run. Power in itself is neither good nor bad. It's not honorable or evil in itself. It's simply the force that makes things happen. What these things are depends on how that power is used. Without power, there is nothing to drive the life. With the power, there is everything to drive the life, to make it do and make it be what we want, what we decide.

Power goes with events and circumstances too. They can be positive or negative, depending on how we allow them to control our own life power. Some events have affected us in ways that made us better. We allowed them to influence our power in ways we wanted. Some events have influenced our power in ways we have not wanted. Viet Nam in particular, has had a great influence on our personal lives, our personal power to be what we want to be. I think you see what I'm trying to say.

We remember and memorialize the power of brothers being killed and missing in Viet Nam. For those who haven't come to terms with it, that power is hard to live with. It's even traumatic and overwhelming. For some of us, it influences way too much our power to be what we want to be. For you who have come to terms with it, the event is still one of great power. But that power has influenced you in ways that have made you a stronger and wiser man. This event has changed our lives as vets because it was of such magnitude that our power was adjusted to how we experienced it and how we wanted it to affect our personal power. Sometimes we might think that only those out in the bush had their personal power affected so much. But that isn't true. Any who served in the rear know the power of the event too. I don't have time to prove it, but think of the graves registration people, think of the nurses and doctors (and medics too). Think of the viewpoint of the rear-ender—he didn't know who was the VC and who was the friendly. Get my drift?

Remembering the men and women we were dependent on during those stressful days impacts your personal power. How can a wounded trooper whose life is saved by a nurse at the field hospital not be changed because of his gratitude for her unselfish dedication to him? How can a chaplain not be changed by remembering the young soldier who asked him to move over so the soldier could have the helicopter's seat of danger in case we took fire? How could the gunner not be changed when he remembers the supply sergeant who kept him in food, ammo, mail, and an M-60 machine gun that worked when he needed it? How can we not be changed in our personal power just by thinking about those we became close to, many of whom did not return?

What about our families? Those we left behind when we went off to war? The power of their presence (or absence) back home was profound. Much of our depth of character came by just knowing someone was at home who cared and let us know it through letters, care packages, or maybe a MARS call. I recognize that many were devastated by the Dear John letter received right after a rugged firefight or day of being point in triple canopy jungle. Some had no family who cared. For these, the power was hard, but the refining process of overcoming produced a maturity of character that I have seen passed on to kids and grandkids, even today.

A great power of healing is present at The Wall, at reunions, in outreach groups and many other places. This power can heal the wounds and scars from Viet Nam that came at such a young age when you were just getting a handle on your personal power and maturity. Much has been said about PTSD and healing of vets, families, and the nation. For those who've stuffed, who've been wounded and who've given so much of your personal power I want you to know there is restoration of personal power through healing and there is joy in knowing it. I've seen it with many vets. I've seen it with many families. It's great to behold! The scars and wounds run deep. The stuff is jammed well. The stories are as varied as the vets. But the healing is there. It's within your power to have.

There's enormous healing when you, as a refined-by-fire vet, get outside yourself and reach out to others. As you help your brothers heal through offering yourself, you gain the power of healing for yourself as well. It works. As your body gains power through exercise and your mind gains power through learning, so your character gains power through using knowledge and understanding produced in you through the fires of war. That is certainly one of your most difficult trials, but it can become one of your most significant opportunities.

There are other sources of power. There is power in the sacrifice of those killed, wounded, or missing in action. There is power in being a survivor, even if it didn't make sense that you survived. There is power in giving service wherever you see it's needed. There is power in opening up, in deliberately remembering and dealing with long-stuffed memories. There is power in sharing wisdom and knowledge. For instance, many young kids really want to know about Viet Nam. Only the vet can really tell them. There's power in your love of America, love of oppressed people, love for your family, and love for your buddies, your brothers that you shared your life's most powerful event with.

I hope you realize that our greatest power is that of God. That's where our life's power comes from to start with. After all, it's God who made us and gave us the purpose for which we were even born. God is the source of power that produces the complete healing we all need. God has a plan for your life. He knows you by name and loves you beyond understanding. He said that he will never leave you or forsake you, which I talked about in another chapter. This includes that he did not abandon you in Viet Nam. Don't forget, God did not start that war. People did. Just because God let people do something evil in the extreme does not mean that he abandoned you. Because he didn't. He was there with you then and he's with you now. That's a source of power you shouldn't miss.

If want to know about real power, which I hope you do, read about it in God's Word, the Holy Bible, Ephesians 1:15-2:10. It talks about God's "incomparably great power for us who believe. That power is like the working of His mighty strength which He exerted in Christ when He raised Him from the dead and seated Him at His right hand...." I don't have space to quote the whole passage. I hope you'll go to Wal Mart or Barnes & Noble and get a modern translation of the Bible, the NIV or something, and read this. You'll see what I mean about power, the driving force for life.

There's a whopping lot that neither you, me or anyone else can understand 100 percent. But what I do understand is that God is over it all. He has 100 percent power and authority. Through Jesus Christ His Son, he has made the way to himself, eternal life, and complete power. Total healing and purpose is available for the taking through belief in him. God's power is our source for the power, the driving force for our life, for our life as it was meant to be from the beginning, with or without Viet Nam.

30

the "a" word

THE "A" WORD IS A B-A-A-A-D WORD. WE DON'T LIKE IT. It offends us. It makes us mad to think about it.

In every society there are certain words people just don't like for whatever reason. The meanings and implications turn them off. I think we all know what the "F" word is. I'm sure not going to explain it here! It's a word not accepted in "polite" society so we say "F" and everyone gets the point, and no one gets their ears scorched.

In Viet Nam vet circles (and plenty of other places too) there's a similar word to the bad word we're talking about here. It has more than four letters but it's a quick turn-off anyway. I'm leading up to telling you what it is, but I want to make sure you keep reading after I tell you. Keep your mind open. Now I'll explain. Are you ready? OK. Here it is: the "A" word is authority. Yes, AUTHORITY.

Now that you're turned off, please turn back on again. I assure you the word is not as harsh or as bad as you may think from your Viet Nam days (or your childhood days, or your jail-house days). Of course, I remember the "——— Lifers." Yes, I knew of plenty of times when the "authority" about got us killed. Yes, some green lieutenants came in, shoved their authority around, and got us into some real deep stuff. Yes, it was those authorities in Washington that got us into this to start with. Yes, my old man kicked me around at home and now "no one's ever going to tell me what to do again."

Trouble is, that's only one part of the issue of authority, and a pessimistic, downbeat one at that. True as it is, it's not the whole picture. Not even the big part.

Think about it. "No one's going to tell me what to do!" No one? What about yourself? Just saying that is exercising authority, self-authority. And some of us aren't doing too well at it. If all this I-can-do-it-my-way, don't-need-no-one, no-one's-going-to-get-inside-of-me attitude is so terrific, then why are we having so much PTSD, so many family crises, so many walls that no one really wants around him or her?

On the other hand, self-authority is a very powerful force and extremely positive and productive when guided and developed well and properly. No one knows you like you do. No one has ever had your experiences in just the way you have. You are unique. God made you as yourself. He either directed or allowed you to have your situations, and he made you for a purpose with a plan. And, as the bumper sticker says, "God don't make junk" (not original). So you are the one and only expert human authority on who you are, where you came from, what you are capable of, and what you are going to contribute to your fellow man. That is powerful, positive, and exciting. It applies to everyone, especially the vet.

There is other authority too. What I said about you also applies to the other guy. He has the same authority over himself as you do over yourself. Just different (so who wants two of the same?). Now, you respect his authority and he respects yours. You talk, listen, learn, agree, disagree, compromise. Pretty soon you're doing a lot more than you ever could do alone toward accomplishing whatever you agreed to do.

Next you come together at a reunion or whatever, and do the same thing. Like at reunions where I'm chaplain. Like, we've accomplished a whole lot just because we shared ourselves, our "expertise" and our authority. Or should I say authorities, plural. After all, think about what authority is, to begin with. By definition. Seems to me it means you're smart about something and can do something about it. So, sometimes someone else has authority over you. So what? Maybe they're smarter than you about something where you both have an interest. Like in a firefight, someone has to tell someone else who to shoot at. Admittedly, authority is way too often abused (try Washington, DC). But the principle still holds. It doesn't work to turn off on all authority, even your own, because of some jerk who got someone killed and it shouldn't have happened. That's right, it shouldn't have happened. Period. Now what?

Don't forget your family. This opens up a whole arena we'll save for later because it's a big subject worthy of discussion. But your family is an authority on being married to a vet, or being the parent or sibling of a vet, or the friend of a vet, or employer, or partner, or *child* of a vet. They know more about what it's like to live with you, or to be your friend, etc., than anyone else. They are the expert and they are the authority. They may not, and probably do not, have the power to force you into submission to their authority. But they still are the authority. It's based on expertise, not power. Authority based on expertise rather than power is far more effective and productive. So listen, learn, and then submit voluntarily. It's not as dangerous as you think. You might even like it.

This leads me to my closing thoughts, which are now. (I always save the best for last.) Jesus Christ said in the Gospel of Matthew 28:18, "All authority in heaven and on earth has been given to me." I take enormous comfort in knowing that the whole world doesn't depend on my personal expertise or authority for its well-being. Thank God, just my own personal life doesn't depend only on my own authority. Life is too big and complicated for me to have to figure it all out on my own.

God is for real. He is the final authority. He is infinite Love, Justice, Mercy, and Forgiveness. He has a plan for my life. He has a plan for your life. As you voluntarily submit to his authority, you'll find your own authority coming together as you never dreamed possible.

Got it?

31

losing your way

ONE DAY IN 1969 I WAS STANDING IN THE SQUADRON
TOC (Tactical Operations Center, for you civilians). As
usual, our recon troops were out busting jungle and going
through the rubber plantations around Loc Ninh. Our S-3
was communicating over the radio with one of the troop
commanders. Don't bother asking me which one, because I
can't tell. No need embarrassing anyone after more than
three decades after the fact. Besides, what I'm going to tell
you about the CO and his troop could have happened to a lot
of us. And it did happen to some. As I was about to say, the
S-3 was talking to this troop commander. He was on some
sort of recon mission and from what was being said, it
became apparent that someone was sure confused. The
instructions given by the S-3 and the replies just didn't add
up. S-3 decided to ask the commander where he was. He
could be heard on his radio to be studying his map. The S-3
was studying his map too. Pretty soon it became obvious,
with the predictable verbal reaction by the S-3, that the
trooper was not where he was supposed to be. What was
more, he was not even where he had thought he was. Yes, he
was lost and his whole recon troop with him. I don't remember how many soldiers and ACavs were out there with him,
but there were plenty. He was over on the next hill from

where he had thought he was. He was on the wrong hill. Fortunately, there was no enemy activity at the time and nothing happened, except the CO was embarrassed, especially when he got his xxx reamed out for doing such a xxxx thing!

Sound familiar? It's probably best that you don't cast any stones, though. There aren't too many of us who haven't gotten lost occasionally, ourselves. Of course, it's not every day that someone gets lost and endangers the lives of many others as can happen in combat. You can get a lot of people hurt real bad. But, to get on with my story, I consider myself a good driver and map reader. When my wife and I were traveling around the USA in our fifth-wheel trailer, I could get us almost anywhere so long as I had a good road map. I remember once, though, when I got into a speck of trouble by trying to get along on my own while ignoring my trusty map. My trouble was compounded because I was driving late at night and was dogtired. Have you ever driven late at night for 150 miles in exactly the opposite direction from where you thought you were heading? I have. Up in Montana. It's humiliating. (It helps your wife keep her sense of humor, though, after she stops chewing you out and starts laughing instead.)

Of course, there are plenty of ways to get lost. Not all of them involve maps either—military, topographical, highway, or whichever. Too many of our brothers, and some of our sisters too, got lost in Viet Nam and didn't find their way, even after they came home. Most didn't exactly come home to cries of, "Welcome Home." Too many thought booze, drugs, hiding in the woods, or stuffing their feelings was the return route back to the world. They were wrong. They were on the wrong hill. Some are still there. Many maps are available to get on track. The maps are of every sort. I'm talking figuratively, as you can see. I'm saying that for those troopers who haven't come all the way home yet, there are plenty of resources available to show the way. I'm not just talking about a bunch of airheads, either. Plenty of vets are around who have been down the same road as you and know the way. They can help. Same as the S-3 who got our troop commander back where he needed to be. Where he needed to be just happened to be where he wanted to be too—and where he was the safest.

In case you've been to reunions, I expect you've met troopers who've traveled the road home. I know they're around because I know many. If you've checked and didn't find someone who could show you the road, try again. It's worth the effort. If you're a vet, a trooper, who's found the way home, be alert for those who are still roaming. There are still plenty wandering around looking for someone who knows the way home.

For those who never got lost in the first place, congratulations! You are most fortunate. There are even those who came home to welcoming committees of supportive family and friends. However, it's too bad, but hardly anyone came home to a welcoming band or parade put on by grateful citizens. Still, many of us had supportive families, friends, churches, or someone that helped a lot. These among us were very fortunate. Let's each of us hold out a road map for those of our brothers and sisters who haven't found their way yet.

After talking to a lot of vets, especially Viet Nam vets, and travelling the road myself, I can make a few suggestions about markers along the way. Finding another caring vet who has come home and talking with him is a good start. Many are available who do understand. There are great support groups out there such as Point Man Ministries. They're a group of Christian vets ministering to other vets. I have supported and participated with them as chaplain in several states. I know they are caring, understanding, and can help show the way home. They are mostly Viet Nam vets. Then there are caring professional agencies out there too. I spent two months in the Black Hills of South Dakota. The VA Hospital in Sturgis has a PTSD team that is great. I knew Viet

Nam vets who came a long way just to see this team. Their guidance has helped show the way home for many.

So, for those of us who have come home, be glad. Enjoy! Regardless of when you made it back, now you can be available to help show the way to others who are still looking. For those still travelling, don't stop. The road home is there. It's narrow, but it's firm and straight. It's worth getting on.

I'll sign off now by pointing out that there *is* a final way home. One day we'll each come to the end of this journey. We'll each come to the end of the road. From where I am now, living in a motor home full time, the end of the road is easy to see. If you're going to make the last and eternal welcome home, you need to recognize the words of the ultimate direction-giver and mapmaker. That is the person of Jesus Christ, the Son of God. What he said on the subject is, "I am the way, the truth, and the life…" (John 14:6). Think about it. I'm travelling the road. So are others. I know my destination. It's my last and best "Welcome Home." After Viet Nam I was welcomed home by my family and some friends. I also was ignored by other family, friends, and people important to me. So my homecoming was mixed: some welcome, some not welcome. But at the end of the road when it really counts, I am assured of the final "Welcome Home." I've read the map. I know the way. I'm on the right road. Come along, the road is open for you too.

32

forgetting

FORGET IT. JUST FORGET IT!

Why don't you just forget it and get on with your life?

Forget her. She isn't worth it.

Forget him. He isn't worth it.

It was a long time ago. Forget it.

It isn't important. Forget it.

Forget it. Act like it never happened.

Let it go. It doesn't matter. Forget it.

Do any of these statements sound familiar? Has anyone ever said it to you? Forgetting isn't always so easy, is it? Some events in life are not easily put out of mind. Sometimes even trivial ones stay in our memories. Since this is true, the more powerful, the more important, the more traumatic events are sure going to stick with us. Some things we do forget. Some stronger ones stay in our conscious memory most of the time. Others stay buried until one day something happens that triggers a memory that might be way more than three decades old.

Many events are insignificant and forgotten, which they should be. They aren't worth remembering. Many are so important or powerful that we can't forget them. Of things we remember and things we forget some are helpful and some are not. Some are downright destructive. These include memories and flashbacks that can bring on a big dose of PTSD. PTS (Post Traumatic Stress) is a normal reaction to an abnormal event. The D part of PTSD is stress that goes beyond normal and becomes incapacitating. Forget it? It would be nice. But I don't know it's going to happen.

When you landed at Tan Son Nhut or Cam Ranh Bay in Viet Nam, you got off the plane and walked out onto the hot tarmac. You were scared and didn't know from nothing what was going to happen. You were the cherry. You were green. The sights and smells were foreign and different to you. Remember the masses of cyclos, bicycles, pull-carts, and exhaust-spewing Lambrettas? You were apprehensive and nervous. How are you going to forget all that?

After a hard day patrolling, busting jungle, flying missions into hot LZs, humping pro-jos or patching up torn bodies at the aid station, you get to take a break and relax. You talk it over with a buddy. You get a care package from home. Your R and R orders came through when you thought the clerk had lost them. You're the clerk, and your grunt buddies said thanks for doing their paperwork right the first time. How are you going to forget that?

You go through hell with a squad of your buddies. You get real tight with each other because you survived several firefights and ambushes. You know all about each other's strengths and weaknesses. You know all about their families and their homes, where they came from and what they did. You know them better than your own brother. Then one day it happens. You're in a real bad one. Several of your buddies are hit. A couple are killed. Several are medevaced out. And, thankfully, most survived, you think. Trouble is, they're shipped out and you never hear of them again. How do you forget that?

One day, over twenty years later, you walk into a reunion and see an old buddy from Viet Nam that you thought was dead. You go to him and hug him. He tells you that yes, you were right, the helicopter did go down after you DEROSed.

Everyone on board was killed and burned. "But I wasn't on board that day." What a great reunion! How do you forget that?

You served on the ground. But you sure did appreciate those jet jockeys who saved your hide many times when the VC and NVA were all over the place and you learned what fear was all about. Then those jets came out of nowhere and made sure the enemy couldn't get to you anymore. Later you served at Bien Hoa or Da Nang and got to know some of those pilots personally because you got a rear job and associated with them. Then some got shot down over North Viet Nam and were taken POW. Or your buddy on the ACav was left when you had to back out of an ambush. When you returned for him he was gone—POW. A helicopter went down in dense and remote jungle. It was never found. Everyone was declared MIA. How do you forget these guys? You don't. We do not forget our POWs and MIAs.

There are some things we just do not forget. Maybe we should forget, sometimes, anyway. But we can't. The event, the experience, was too powerful. It burned into our memory. Some things we do not want to forget. Our brothers we served with are so much a part of our lives. They deserve to be remembered. Our KIAs we remember with the honor and respect that they earned. Our POWs deserve to be remembered because the price and burden they bear is so heavy. They also deserve whatever we and our country can do to get them back—*all* of them. Our MIAs because they were our brothers and are a part of us. All of their families and loved ones because they are a part of us also. Why would we forget any of these?

Are we supposed to forget the power of our past? Should we forget what made us who we are today? I don't think so. What about the traumas that overwhelm us and bring on the PTSD? I'm not sure that forgetting is the answer. Why try to force what really can't be done, anyway. Maybe the better answer is to handle these matters well, to put memories into perspective, to make the past a matter of our history and go on from there. That history was powerful, personal, and real. But it is still history and that's not where we live.

For the positive memories, the events of our history, we are richer. For the friends we made, the actions we performed that made us better, made Viet Nam better and made our country better, we are grateful. We matured. We learned. We loved. I can tell you about orphanages, hospitals, MED-CAPS, kids thronging GIs for candy, old people smiling at Americans going through their Cambodian village, of love and sacrifice between soldiers, of a life given for another. I can tell you about VC using women and children as human shields during Tel '68 because they knew that Americans would not shoot at women and children, regardless of what the media would have you believe.

Without a doubt, many negatives are particularly hard to handle. Some things done are too gross to be specific here. You know what I mean. Many of us have vivid pictures of suffering, shock, horror, mutilation etched on our brains that will not go away by just saying "forget it." Many of us did forget it for decades and now much of what was stuffed is coming up again. So it's not so easy to just forget as we might like.

So now what? I realize it's a lot easier to give advice than to take it. This includes giving advice to yourself and taking it. Just the same, there are things we need to do. I'm not smart enough to know it all, but here are some things I see as true and helpful:

Some memories must be made a part of your history. They happened long ago. Seeing them as only yesterday is happening with of a lot of vets, but it accomplishes absolutely nothing except to bring on a lot of misery. You cannot undo what was done and you cannot will yourself to forget. You cannot erase it. But you can fill your life and your mind with so much positive that it crowds out the bad. It leaves no room for it. Covering it with booze and drugs is not what I mean. That only makes matters worse. A lot worse.

We must set clear priorities in our lives. We must see our families, our wives, our kids, and loved ones as more important than our memories, no matter how vivid they are. We must see our present and future as separate from our past. We learn from our past and build on it. But we leave the past behind us and move forward even while we acknowledge that things happened. They just happened, past tense. And that's where we leave them—in the past. War is hell. We know that. No one would have said it was hell if it wasn't. It sure wasn't glorious, no matter what you expected before you went.

I want to say something I believe very deeply and hope you take to heart. There are many among us who truly did reprehensible things which cannot be forgotten. Some did things for which they are profoundly sorry. I know many stories that are ugly beyond belief. I know of incidents from being close by during my two combat tours in Viet Nam. I know of incidents told to me directly by those involved. All of us, for one matter or another, have an overpowering need to experience forgiveness. I believe that one of the hardest things for many vets to do is to accept forgiveness. The ugliness of memories may not be erased from our minds, but they can be defeated by the simple yet profound action of accepting forgiveness. You may need the forgiveness of your wife and your kids. You may need to accept the forgiveness of your buddies or their families. Way above that, though, you do need to seek and accept the forgiveness of Almighty God, your highest power. Some things can't be forgiven by our brothers or our family. They go way beyond them. But *nothing* goes beyond what God can, and will, forgive. Trust me, God didn't make provision only for your small or medium sins and wrong actions like stealing a tank of gas or smoking a joint on guard duty. He provided the sacrifice of his Son on the cross to cover your biggest, ugliest sins. The ones you cannot handle and cannot forget. These I don't have to list because you know. You're not alone, though. Consider the

Apostle Paul, who was one of the main men in the Bible. He committed ugly atrocities against innocent people that you would hardly believe. Later he was forgiven and it changed him into a whole new man. He wrote that God "has rescued us from the dominion of darkness and brought us into the kingdom of the Son he loves, in whom we have redemption, the forgiveness of sins" (Colossians 1:13-14).

When you are forgiven, it means the matter is not held against you any longer. The matter is over and done with. This doesn't mean results don't happen. Because what happened, happened. Forgiveness won't make the situation original and won't change history. But forgiveness wipes the slate clean and gives a whole new start. Got it?

I offer you these thoughts from my heart. I hope we all learn to keep our memories in perspective. Even if we can't forget, we can, by God's grace, learn to keep everything in perspective. So let's keep our history in the past. Let's learn and grow from our history. Sometimes we must be forgiven. Maybe we can even make atonement. But the present is now and the future is ahead. Let's concentrate on using our past to make the present and future brighter and better. Can we forget? I doubt it. Can we go from here renewed and recharged? Yes, we can. No doubt about it.

33

role model

RIDING WITH THE BLACKHORSE IN VIET NAM PRODUCED many memories, some great, some not so great, some long-lasting, some quickly forgotten. Some memories are of incidents that burned themselves into our brains, some are filled with indescribable terror, some are of times that were actually fun. Some memories are about people who made an impression we can't forget. Some people we would like to forget; there are turkeys everywhere, after all. Some of these who made lasting impressions were our buddies. Others were leaders we looked up to and honestly trusted. Some leaders we even saw as role models because they did their job very well and they actually cared deeply for their soldiers. You could see it. Whether they were common or rare is your business to decide. You knew both kinds. So did I.

I'll tell you about one who truly loved his soldiers and took care of them very well while doing his job of fighting the war in the jungles of Viet Nam and Cambodia. He was our squadron S-3. I didn't tell him I was going to tell this story because he might be reluctant, as if it were bragging. He is such a decent, unassuming man. To me, he's a role model of dedication, compassion, and wisdom. A lot of us know him. He was the type of leader who was always out with the men—not the type who hung around the safe areas telling

155

everyone else where to go. There were others who would fly in after a firefight and write themselves up for a medal (or have someone else do it for them). S-3 was not like that in any way. You could count on him.

I know he won't mind if I tell you about something that happened to him that I thought was pretty funny. He used to fly around in a LOCH, that egg-shaped scout helicopter that could fly anywhere. Fred was his pilot this particular day. (We had great pilots, too. They loved S-3 and didn't mind telling me about their exploits with him.) Anyway, this particular day, they were flying over the rubber (a rubber tree plantation) near Loc Ninh and S-3 somehow managed to drop his map out of the helicopter. I don't need to tell you, that could cause us a passel of trouble if the VC or NVA got hold of it. So what did Fred the Pilot and S-3 do about it? I'm sure you're smart enough to know that most would have dee-dee maued (spelling?) out of there. Your normal S-3 would probably have called for some ground troops to retrieve the map, if they could even find it before Charlie did. However, Fred the Pilot took that LOCH down between the rubber trees, which practically touched each other and landed. S-3 got out, retrieved the map, Fred the Pilot maneuvered up between the rubber trees, and they proceeded on their merry way. And I mean *merry* way. True story. By the way, S-3 was a major. I don't mind telling major stories. I tell stories about everyone else. Why not majors too?

Now, to proceed with this story and why S-3 is one of my role models. The day we went into Cambodia, 1 May 1970 according to my recollection, S-3, along with Squadron CO, Regimental CO, and Squadron CSM, went into Cambodia *on the ground*. If you know how things operated back then, you know that *on the ground* was very significant. Frankly, that was unheard of. In an operation of that magnitude and danger, the brass almost always commanded from the air, as in from a helicopter where they could see better, but were also safer. I'm not knocking that. It was usually necessary. I'm just pointing this out to you to show the caliber of the leadership we had at that place and time. Since S-3 is the subject of this story, we'll stick with the subject. S-3 rode on one of our ACavs. I wasn't on the spot at the time: I was on another spot at the time. Same jungle, different spot. But I heard this story very soon: it seems that S-3 along with Regimental CO, Squadron CSM, and one of our troopers were doing something with a VC or NVA officer, like trying to take him prisoner. Anyway, as I understand it, the NVA somehow managed to chuck a hand grenade out with his free hand. Naturally, grenades don't care who threw it or who's the target. They just explode where they land. That's what happened. S-3 and Regimental CO took the brunt of the explosion. It was near Snoul. I think in the rubber there. A lot happened in the rubber. Remember my story about rubber flies? They were funny. This hand grenade explosion was not funny. S-3 and Regimental CO were severely wounded and medevaced out, naturally.

I visited S-3 and Regimental CO at the evac hospital at Long Binh. I think it was the next day. I think it was the 24th Evac Hospital. But who can remember numbers so long ago? Regimental CO took shrapnel all up and down the front of his body. They wanted to evac him to Japan. He wouldn't go. He was in the 24th Evac Hospital for two weeks and went back to the Blackhorse where he figured he belonged. He must have been right because he eventually wound up a great career as a four-star general. His name was, and still is, Donn Starry.

S-3 had to be evacuated to Japan. He lost a leg just below the knee, as I recall. It took a long time to heal. I think a couple of years. I didn't see him again for a long time. But he was one determined and dedicated man. I understand that when "they" wanted to medically retire him, he refused it and fought it within the system. I don't know the details of how he did it, but I do know that he won because he stayed on active duty and I followed his career through mutual acquaintances.

Being a chaplain for twenty-seven years was long enough to renew many acquaintances. One of the most exciting was seeing S-3 again, minus a leg, in Germany. Actually, you couldn't tell the leg was gone because he had such a great prosthesis. He still has it, of course. Anyway, this time he was the Regimental CO in Fulda, Germany, not Cambodia or Viet Nam. And that's not the half of it. (I'm making this story real short.) Do you remember Desert Storm? Remember the flanking movement by VII Corps around the Iraqi forces that went around to their west and cut them off at the pass which was the road back to Baghdad? Anyway, that Corps commander loved his troops. He did a lot to win that war. He treated his troops right and also won. How can you beat that? He was a three-star general by that time. You've probably guessed who it was and you're right. The three star was S-3. End of story you say? Not! The last time I saw S-3, I was still in the Army stationed at Ft. Huachuca, Arizona. We were under TRADOC. Guess who the four-star commander was by then. You're right again. It was S-3. Sure was great to see him after all those years and all that history in between. He hadn't changed a bit, except for all those stars on his shoulders and a mustache. He still loved his soldiers and still does. Only now his soldiers are vets. At reunions the brothers know what he's like. Many have met him. His name is Fred Franks.

Fred would be embarrassed for me to tell his story like this. That's partly because he's such a great role model. He's humble but not bashful. He's a great example of how character and virtue can drive a person's life. Hard work, dedication to his principles, love of his family, love of his fellow soldiers and love of God, his highest power.

There's another reason, though, that Fred wouldn't mind me telling his story and using him as a role model: because it helps make the point that every one of us is a role model too. In case you thought there was a typo or you didn't understand, I said, *every one of us is a role model.* That includes *you.* You are a role model for someone. It's perfectly possible for you to be a *negative* role model. That's true. But you don't have to be negative. For the record, no one is perfect, including you and me. But you're a role model for someone, just the same. If you have kids and you love them, then you're teaching them to love. If you beat on them or you beat on your wife, you're teaching them to do the same. If you have grandkids, the same applies. If you have PTSD, or if you did have it, then you're a role model for other vets on how to handle it—or how to not handle it. Get it? Someone is watching you. Even if you live under a bridge or if you live in a mansion, someone, somewhere is watching you. Your main decision is what sort of role model you will be. It's partly your decision who you will be a role model for. Only partly. Because whatever people you are around, that's where the principle applies. If you are a hermit, the principle still applies because some people are interested in watching hermits. Comprende?

Now, speaking of perfect people, which we did just a second ago, I do not know how to relate to perfect people. I doubt if you know how either. Fact of the matter is, if I was around someone who thought he was perfect, I would probably have to leave. People who think they're perfect are hard to be around. So don't bother thinking you have to be perfect to be a role model, because people who think they're perfect are terrible role models. Agreed? I think so.

Which brings me to my very last point. That is that the only perfect person, anyway, was Jesus Christ and he was, and is, the Son of God. He was a perfect role model. And you can relate to him that way. That's one of the reasons he came. First, to save us from our sins, which shouldn't be hard to admit to. Then, to show us the way to God Almighty. Then, to show us how to live, which is a very good idea when you come to think of it. A very good idea, even if you hadn't come to think of it. So think of it. After all, Jesus did say, "The thief comes only to steal and kill and destroy; I have come that they may have life, and have it to the full" (John 10:10). I hope you'll think about these things.

34

not alone

DO YOU KNOW WHAT A CANOPY IS? A CANOPY IS AN overhead covering. It's something that's spread out overhead to keep out whatever is above from getting to whatever is below. A canopy can be a canvas covering held up by poles so people can stand under it and be protected from the sun. I remember another kind of canopy. You probably remember the same kind of canopy that I remember. It's a jungle canopy. A jungle canopy has trees so thick and dense that it covers you overhead the same as a canvas canopy at a party would. Except the canvas canopy at a party is to keep the sun off so people will be more comfortable and cool. The canopy in the jungle also keeps the sun off of you. It does a lot more too. I remember one time when we were "covered" by a lot of jungle canopy. I guess it was a three or four layer canopy jungle. Unless you can have five or six layers, then I guess that's what it was. However many layers there were doesn't matter anyway. What matters is that the jungle sure was thick, overhead and along the sides too.

To show you how thick the canopy was, we had hardly any direct sunlight, even at noon, just lots of shade. One time when the squadron commander was flying overhead in his helicopter, he couldn't figure out exactly where we were. We knew where he was because we could hear him. Remember

160

the whop! whop! whop! (or whap! whap! whap!) of the Huey? Viet Nam vets remember the sound of a Huey very well. Matter of fact, just hearing one go over to this day can bring back memories, even flashbacks, for a few of the guys. Anyway, the canopy was so thick overhead that the CO couldn't figure out just where we were. So he said to pop smoke so he could see where we were. So we popped smoke. He still couldn't see where we were because the canopy was so thick it absorbed all the colored smoke crystals before they could get above the trees. So the CO had to get by with knowing *about* where we were.

Why am I telling you this? Well, I thought it would bring back some memories and maybe some would be good, very good. Besides, I have a point to make. I haven't told you yet who the "we" is in my narrative so far. Not that you asked. (If I waited for you to ask we could be here all day.) "We" were a platoon from one of the recon troops I was riding with that day. The jungle was in Cambodia. It was when we were there legally. (Remember the Cambodian Incursion?) We were moving along a jungle "highway," a part of the Ho Chi Minh Trail system. Naturally we were moving in column. Ever try moving on line along a trail ten feet wide? What we were doing was looking for NVA. We found some.

To tell the truth, it was kind of an unnerving place to be. Up ahead another platoon had just blown away some NVA coming toward them in USAID trucks in some sort of a convoy. Can you imagine driving along a jungle trail so narrow you could put your arm out either window, if you had a window, and hit a tree with your fist? Don't try it, the tree will win. But it shows you how narrow the road was. Naturally the NVA didn't survive since the lead vehicle in our little Cav convoy was a Sheridan. As we were going along this jungle highway we came upon an ACav from another troop. The crew was just sitting there. They didn't look too happy. As a matter of fact they looked very *un*happy. As a matter of another fact they looked unhappy, nervous, and a little scared. Not that

Cav troopers ever got scared. Except for me, of course. We asked the troopers what was their problem. Their problem was that their ACav had broken down and the rest of the troop had to go on ahead without them because of the mission. I guess the mission had been to blow away that NVA truck convoy I just told you about. It was toward evening, so we knocked down a lot of jungle growth for a field of fire and set up a night defensive position. Everything was OK.

After all these years, I've never forgotten those guys on that ACav sitting out there all by themselves along that Cambodian jungle trail. Considering the situation, considering where they were, considering that there were plenty of NVA out there that would be very happy to help them to become dead, considering that they were out there by themselves, or so they thought, until we came along, they sure must have felt lonely. And that's the point of this story. A lot of Viet Nam vets out there are still sitting all alone on their own jungle trail. They may be physically sitting behind an office desk, they may be driving an eighteen wheeler, they may behind bars twenty-four hours a day or sitting at a bar every night self-medicating. They may be sleeping under a bridge, they may be playing golf, or they may be holed up in the mountains of Washington state or New Mexico.

How many people are around isn't always what determines how you feel. A lot of people feel intensely lonely in the middle of a crowd or even at their own birthday parties. Let me assure you that you don't have to be a combat vet to feel lonely, either. Plenty of people feel lonely, including rape or crime victims. Some Viet Nam and Blackhorse troopers too. And other vets like WWII, Korea, Desert Storm, Iraqi Freedom, Panama, Somalia, and the others included. If you're lonely, you're lonely. I know. Others know too. You're not the only one who was ever lonely. Why else would so many live in the mountains away from civilization just as if they were still in the 'Nam? I heard there are an estimated four thousand Viet Nam vets holed up in the mountains of Northern Arizona alone. About how we feel, I have this to say: 1. You need to understand 2.Your buddies need you to understand 3.Your family needs you to understand 4.I need you to understand (take your choice of which fits best because all are true) that many times how we *feel* is not how we really *are*. For example, sometimes the most beautiful of women *feel* very ugly. Why they feel that way isn't the point. The point is, that is how they feel and they need someone to help them overcome that bad feeling. Sometimes the devoted love of a committed husband can be a real help. Remember the country and western song, "she doesn't know she's beautiful?" That didn't mean she felt ugly, but it helps make the point, doesn't it?

Feeling lonely is similar. Just because we feel lonely doesn't mean we are alone. And if we really are *alone* it doesn't mean we have to stay that way. Those troopers along the Ho Chi Minh Trail in the Cambodian jungle sure felt alone. And I didn't blame them for feeling that way. There they were, stuck on a broken ACav and couldn't see two feet to the sides or twenty feet down the trail. Sure looked lonely. Sure looked dangerous. Sure looked spooky. And they didn't know if anyone else was around anywhere, including Charlie. What they didn't know was that we were coming up to them. I guess I don't need to tell you how they felt. Like were we ever welcome! Almost like heroes, except we were all in it together. They weren't lonely any more. Still scared, of course. Why should they be any different? But now they didn't have to face the night alone. They didn't have to face the dangers alone. They didn't have to face their fears alone. Because they weren't alone. And you aren't alone either. You may *feel* alone. But that doesn't mean you *are* alone. Because you're *not*. That's what reunions are all about. That's what your buddies are all about, that's what the telephone is for, that's what the internet is for, that's what the e-mail and snail mail are for. It's called communication.

Communicate with someone who cares about you. That person is there. Who? Your Blackhorse brothers, or whatever outfit you served with, and your other Viet Nam vet brothers too. Add your family, your spouse, your kids. (Yes, we're old enough now so that some of us have grown kids. They understand and care. Give them a chance.) Add your pastor, your chaplain, your VA (yes there are some VA vets groups that care), Point Man and other Christian vets ministries that know what they're talking about, your church (yes there are some Christ-centered churches that are reliable and truthful), your AA or other self-help group, the vet next door, and so forth and so on. If you want to be alone, that's your business. The point here is that you do have a choice. I'm not even saying we all have great problems. That wouldn't be true. We're all different. Thank God for that. But we don't *have* to be lonely. Being alone when we are tired or need to get away isn't what I mean. We don't have to be lonely, alone in the world feeling that nobody understands or cares. There are plenty who do understand and who do care. They were there too, y'know.

Not everyone understands or cares. True. So? You don't need everyone to understand. You don't need everyone to care. Just someone. And that someone is there. Don't shut them out. Or maybe I should say, *stop* shutting them out. Understand? I hope so. I think so.

Let me finish with my biggest point, the best for last, remember? I'd appreciate if you'll read the story of Joshua, one of the great warriors of history. It's in the book of Joshua, the sixth book of the Old Testament part of the Bible. Joshua was getting ready to lead the Israelites into the Promised Land. It was to be a dangerous military operation. God told Joshua, "Be strong and very courageous. Be careful to obey all the law my servant Moses gave you; do not turn from it to the right or to the left, that you may be successful wherever you go.... Then you will be prosperous and successful. Have I not commanded you? Be strong and courageous. Do not be terrified; do not be discouraged, for the Lord your God will be with you wherever you go" (Joshua 1:7-9).

I want to remind you that, like the troopers along the Ho Chi Minh Trail in Cambodia, you're not really alone. Regardless of how you may feel, regardless of the difficulty of your experiences, regardless of what happened in Viet Nam, regardless of no welcome home, regardless of anything you can think of, God is still there. Feelings, perceptions, and even personal experience aren't always reliable in determining the presence of God and whether you're alone, which you are not. God said it. Plenty have experienced it. I have. I hope, when you think about it, that you realize it too. God is with you. Jesus proves it.

'Nuff said. Think about it. OK?

35

getting away with it—not!

I REMEMBER MANY STORIES FROM VIET NAM. SOME OF them were really two-sided, like funny and not funny or like good and bad. They say two different things at once. Here's a story I'll tell you so you can see what I mean. This story really happened, by the way.

In 1969 we were on stand-down in the rear at Di An when we heard the IG was coming to inspect us. You remember how it was in those days, things could be pretty loose, especially with units that spent most of their time in the field. People weren't always too official about how they obtained supplies or where they came from. They were more interested in making things happen than always going through channels. Know what I mean? Lots of equipment was "re-appropriated" from other places or through the "midnight requisition" system. There was even a "maverick" jeep here and there. No one could account for this stuff. It was just there because it was needed and it was too hard to get everything by the book. The point isn't about whether it was right or wrong, necessary or unnecessary. That's another point, which gets a bit complicated. We can talk about that later, if you want. I'm coming to the moral of this story in a minute. Keep reading.

We now had all this "extra" stuff that no one could account for by the book. And the bean counters were on the way. I don't remember which, but one of the first sergeants who'd been around for a long time knew how to deal with bean counters, or so he thought. He didn't want to get rid of all the equipment he needed but which he couldn't account for. So he came up with a plan. His plan was this: he got a couple of his Blackhorse troopers and told them what to do. You ask, "Would a Blackhorse trooper do such a thing?" I have to reply, "Yes." What Top said to do was to load all this stuff onto a deuce and a half truck. He told them to just drive around all day and come back in the evening when the IG team was gone. Simple? Yes. Foolproof? I don't think so. Not hardly. The troopers started out doing what the first sergeant told them. However, about two that afternoon, wouldn't you know it, the local MPs were out on patrol and happened to spot a certain deuce and a half loaded with a lot of "stuff" parked in front of the local village brothel. You can figure out the rest of the story. The troopers were caught "with their pants down" and so was the first sergeant (only with Top it wasn't as literal as with his troopers).

This is one of those two-sided stories I told you about. On one hand, I thought it was pretty funny. Actually even if I am a chaplain, I thought it was very funny. What makes this true story two-sided is that it points up a serious side of life. Which is that in this incident the guilty parties didn't get away with what they tried to do. What they tried to do was not legal, although being in a combat situation, the circumstances were certainly mitigated. Especially when you consider how messed up a lot of things were over there. But they still didn't get away with it.

I don't think anything real serious ever came of the incident. A little butt chewing, and that's about all. Except that a lot of people learned a real lesson about honesty and about what you can get away with and what you can't. As I see it, a very important lesson is that every action has a result. In life you can't really get away with anything. No matter what, whatever you do will always cause something else to happen which maybe you wanted and maybe you didn't.

Here's another chaplain story. During my first tour in Viet Nam I was on an airfield at Soc Trang, deep in the Mekong Delta. We had a small infirmary and clinic which had a half dozen beds. In those days rumors circulated about an insidious type of VD that was going around. It was said to be a strain of gonorrhea so resistant to antibiotics that it was incurable and, if you caught it, you couldn't go home. Sometimes I'd walk through the infirmary to see patients. When I'd see a GI lying in uniform on top of the bed with an IV in his arm, he'd give me a sheepish grin knowing that I knew he'd been messing around with the local prostitutes. I'd give him a grin back, and talk about something else, something important like the weather or the stock market. It was really pretty funny, this mind game. We spoke a lot, mainly through body language and understanding. It was another two-sided situation. Funny in a way. But not at all funny in other ways. Like, did VD have a lasting effect on these men? I don't know. Did some of them leave children behind? Yes, some of them did. Is this funny? In no way. Do any of them know whether they left children behind? I doubt it. Did they get away with messing around? Doesn't look like it. Most, maybe all, were probably cured of their VD. But there were other things that happened that were harder to measure. Like guys said it was up to the girl to keep herself clean and un-pregnant. Tell that to the child he left behind.

The main point of this is that you can't get away with anything. Not when all is said and done. Everything we do produces a result. Everything we do leaves a mark. Everything we do leaves the world either a little better or a little worse. Most of us, you and me, measure our results in small terms, except for our family and those we love and who love us too. Then our results are great.

This could get pretty philosophical, but, simply put and like I said, there's no such thing as getting away with anything. Everything we do or say produces a result somewhere, including whatever we did in Viet Nam. It's part of our history. In a nutshell, we can't change the past and the results are equivalent with what happened.

Moving on, I want to be clear that nothing is hopeless. Although our history can't change, the results can change their character by how we handle the follow-up, by what we do about it now. I'll put it in another nutshell because this could go on for a long time. Whatever in your Viet Nam history is great and positive, be glad. You served well and honorably, if you're average. Be glad and hold your head high. On the other hand, whatever you may be sorry for and whatever you may or should regret, make the changes and seek the forgiveness you need. Since you're a man (or woman as the case may be) and not a stone, you can do it. We've talked about it before, but I'll say it again, through forgiveness you can have a clean slate. Get forgiveness from wherever you need it, or from whoever you many have offended, including family, friends, strangers, and mostly, from God.

Going back to my story about the first sergeant and his troopers, they were looking out for their men in a tough war situation. Without judging whether they should have been doing what they were doing, the first sergeant needed to hide the equipment so the IG team wouldn't take it away. Good. The troopers did something in their own interest; they went to the local whorehouse for a good time and got caught. Bad. This whole situation has two sides, with results that were wanted on the one hand and not wanted on the other hand. This is just a small story illustrating how each of us came out of Viet Nam. Some things we did were good and some bad. You fill in the details. For the good I want you to be glad and proud. For the bad, I hope you'll obtain forgiveness and get a fresh start and new outlook. Take this part of your personal history and learn from it. Mature. Teach those coming after you what you learned.

For all of us I want to offer this verse from the Bible because it applies very well and sums up a lot of what I'm trying to say: "Repent, then, and turn to God, so that your sins may be wiped out, that times of refreshing may come from the Lord, and that he may send the Christ, who has been appointed for you—even Jesus" (Acts 3:19-20). God can and will wipe your slate clean. He gives new starts. He'll take the good and use it well. He'll take the bad and wipe it from the record or make it into something strong and even good. You fill in your details and I'll fill in mine. Don't forget. You'll be glad you did.

36

we were young then—they are now

D<small>ID YOU KNOW THAT THE AVERAGE AGE OF SOLDIERS IN</small> Viet Nam was about 19? You already knew that? OK. Not that anyone had to remind you. Just remember back to those days. Better yet, pull out those old snapshots your buddies took over there in the jungle. You looked like a kid. Of course, if you were average (or younger), you really were just a kid. Not that you would have admitted it then. But from your perspective these however-many years later, you see you really were a kid. Of course, fighting the war in Viet Nam made you grow up real fast. On the other hand, some of us were on the high side of that average of 19. I was 30. That made me an old man. Old man at 30? Yeah, I guess so. At least over there. Not that I was alone. Plenty of lifers were my age. A few non-lifers too. Some even older.

Now, here we are, fighting this war on terrorism. Whenever you read this we'll probably still be in it. Maybe it'll get even worse than it is right now. Not worse than 9/11. But worse than now. I hope not. We have a great new generation of young soldiers and I don't think any of us want to see them go over to Afghanistan or Lower Slobbovia or anywhere else to fight any more wars, including terrorism wars. We didn't want to see them go off to Iraq either, but they did. That's what freedom and democracy are all about. Someone has to pay the cost or it's all gone and done. I hope you recognize that the current generation of soldiers is the next generation down from us. In other words, they are our kids. Maybe even our grandkids.

I had an experience a while back that pointed this out to me. I got to thinking about how time goes so fast, how "we get too soon old and too late schmart." Ever hear that one before? Yes? So you know what I mean. I went over to Fort Irwin when I was in Southern California visiting family and my old stomping grounds. That's where the National Training Center is located. You already knew that? So then you know what I'm talking about. I drove my forty-foot diesel motor home there and parked behind regimental headquarters. No, I didn't sneak in. How could I? It's almost as loud as a tank, even though a lot more comfortable. It's where I live (with my wife) and they invited me to park it there for a few days. Nice guys. They treated me very well. Like they really appreciate Viet Nam vet troopers. We (you) are real role models for them. They look up to you (us). But then, we're like their dads to them. Or at least like their dad's generation. Seems like I said something like this a minute ago, didn't I?

One of our troopers from our Viet Nam days was there too. He was treated very well, as I was. I think they even had an officer escort him around. He was a real VIP. They actually let him sleep in the field with the troops. "You're kidding", you say? You say, "what?" No they didn't order him to go out to the field. How could they? He's a civilian now. He went out overnight because he wanted to. He asked for it. I didn't see him the next day, but I think he wanted to do it for the experience and the memories. Maybe to feel young again too. After all, these kids were the same age as he was when he was in the Nam. Besides, even though they were in the field with the hardships and dirt, no one was shooting at them for real. Big difference. Much better, right? Right.

"Did I go out overnight too", you ask? Well, actually, no. What I did was to go out all day starting at 0600 hours (That's 6:00 A.M., remember?), which was most of what brought all this to mind. I was out there with these great young soldiers who looked exactly like y'all did back in those Viet Nam days. Speaking of bringing back old memories! However, they weren't you and we weren't back in the Nam. We were at the National Training Center in the Mojave Desert.

That leads me to something else that really drove home to me. Want to hear it? (You can always skip this part—but then you'd never know what I was going to say). I spent the whole day riding around in a Humvee. Let me tell you, Humvees are sure a lot better than jeeps. Guess whose Humvee I was riding around in. You'd never guess, so I'll tell you. It was the *Command Sergeant Major's* Humvee. I will resist getting sidetracked here because my point is the Regimental Command Sergeant Major. And my point with him is that he was a PFC in Germany when I was there *after* I left Viet Nam. He wasn't old enough to be a Blackhorse trooper in Viet Nam, especially not during the early years, including the boat ride over in '66. Now here he is, the enlisted ole man of the regiment. And he's a lot younger than me (always will be, too). Probably younger than you too, but that's a close call.

Now here we are, more than three decades later. Those young troopers are out there in that desert, whereas we were over there in that jungle. All for the same purpose of keeping this great land of ours free and what we want it to be. The Blackhorse patch is still proud and visible. Mostly it's proud because of the reputation we gained for it in Viet Nam. We continued a proud tradition from the early days of the century and WWII. Desert Storm kept it going. Now our regiment is at the NTC, training the Army and keeping our traditions alive, well, and proud. The success of Iraqi Freedom proves my point. The troopers of today's generation look up to our generation just like we looked up to our dad's WWII generation. Now we look in the mirror and wonder what happened. We may get out an old uniform and realize it doesn't fit any more, except for some of you fortunate skinny guys. That's when we realize that time really does move on. Generations come and generations go. Ours was a "dynamite" generation. It still is. We contributed far more than people knew at the time. History and the march of time have proven the value of the Viet Nam vet. We are a great bunch. So is the current generation of troopers. They're proving their value too. And they look to us as role models and heroes, believe it or not. That's what I've seen with my own eyeballs wide open.

Some day we'll be gone. I'll tell you for sure, though, we'll not be forgotten. We've made our mark. As far as I'm concerned, this country of ours, the good ole US of A, is a lot better because the Blackhorse rode through. It's still riding. We're still making our mark. Only now there's a new generation on board.

I'll close off with a section of the Bible that is appropriate about how time passes on. It's from the Old Testament book of Psalms chapter 103 and verses 13-18: "As a father has compassion on his children, so the Lord has compassion on those who fear him [fear means what it says plus respect, honor, reverence and love]; for he knows how we are formed, he remembers that we are dust. As for man, his days are like grass, he flourishes like a flower of the field; the wind blows over it and it is gone, and its place remembers it no more. But from everlasting to everlasting the Lord's love is with those who fear him, and his righteousness with their children's children—with those who keep his covenant and remember to obey his precepts."

Well, like my folks used to say, time goes faster the older you get. Now here I am, in my sixties and doggone if Dad wasn't right. It's good to see that the Blackhorse is still "in the saddle." But, mostly it's good to see that God is still "on the throne." When all is said and done and even the young generation has grown old, God will still be on the throne, God will still be where you are, God will still be providing for our life's purpose and our soul's salvation through his son, Jesus the Christ, just like he is now. And if events of the past are any indication, a mission will always be there for you, me, the Blackhorse and the generations that come after.

37

freedom birds

CONTINENTAL AIRLINES, STEWARDESSES, TECH SER-geants, LBJ, 365th day, World Airways, turning in your gear, waiting, sitting backwards, brown-bag lunches, adios amigos (goodbye friends). When you take them all together, what do you get? Here's a hint which is pretty strange, but stick with me and you'll get it: these things all have to do with a certain kind of bird. Now, how many kinds of birds can you name? Hawks and doves, of course, as any Viet Nam vet recalls. Also pheasants to shoot, chickens to eat, pigeons to poop, jailbirds to avoid being one of, bird colonels to salute (unless you're one, then you return the salute), birds to flip (chaplains aren't supposed to know about these and anyway you could get your head knocked off for flipping the bird at someone bigger than you). My hint is pretty strange, I'll admit, but I wanted you to think of different kinds of birds. Then I think you'll agree that what I described is a bird. However, not just any bird, but our absolute favorite bird of all time. Here's the bird—*Freedom Bird*. Now don't tell me that's not your favorite kind of bird. But if you don't know what that is, then you must not have been in the 'Nam and you should go ask a 'Nam vet about Freedom Birds. He (or she) will most definitely tell you.

I'll tell you about my experience with Freedom Birds because I think that'll stimulate your own memory of them.

After all, everybody over there had one—a Freedom Bird, that is. Even those of you who got hit and medevaced out had a special kind of Freedom Bird.

Some of us went out of country from Cam Ranh Bay or somewhere up north where I've never been. Others like me went out where we came in, which was Tan Son Nhut Air Base and LBJ. LBJ doesn't mean Lyndon Baines Johnson or Long Binh Jail. This LBJ was Long Binh Junction! For those who missed it, that was the processing center for going in and out of country for a lot of soldiers, including yours truly. There's a lot about leaving Viet Nam the first time that I don't even remember, some things being easier to forget than others. What I do remember very well is this: After sitting around for hours waiting to go home, it came into sight. You might ask, "What came into sight?" Its tail. "What?" you say. I'll answer like this: I'll never forget the beauty of the tail on that Continental Airlines 707 while it moved along behind other planes as it *slowly* came our way, the tail being all I could see at the time. Then that beautiful *Freedom Bird* came around another plane and the whole plane, that whole Freedom Bird, came completely into view. What a magnificent sight! No one cared whether it was Continental, TWA, World or Pan Am. It was a wonderful airplane! It was our own personal Freedom Bird come to get us! After the scared, green new-guys disgorged (got out) we climbed aboard, took off and were on our way home! Back to the folks and the land of the Big PX. Back to where we belonged. Out of the war. Freedom! 365 days of fear and jungle-busting over with. Life in the war zone was over, finished, *feenee*. We were changed men. Little did we realize just how much we had changed. That all came out later. For now, it was freedom! And that beautiful Freedom Bird was going to take us there! What joy! What excitement! What anticipation!

My second tour Freedom Bird was a little different. This is where tech sergeants, brown-bag lunches, World Airways, C141s and sitting backwards come in. For my first tour I had

been in the Mekong Delta with helicopters. We celebrated Tet
'68 that year—some of you remember that "party." Our
Freedom Bird had been just what we'd looked forward to for
a year: a real civilian airliner with all the amenities, such as
stewardesses. This time I was coming out of the jungles along
the Cambodian border with the Blackhorse, the 11th
Armored Cavalry Regiment, the *real* cav! Back to LBJ. What
a drab place it was when processing *into* country. What a
great place it was processing *out* of country. All a matter of
perspective. And my perspective had changed over that year,
that year of my wild ride with the great Blackhorse.

We were processed out and ready for our Freedom Bird
to come and take us home. I'd given back my jungle fatigues
and everything else they said we had to turn in. The jungle
fatigues got washed and sent back out to the field. That's
where yours came from when you were in the field. Did you
know that? I guess someone in the rear got the new
fatigues—who knows? Who cares? We even had to turn in
our flashlights. We could keep only our jungle boots.
Remember? But who cared? Not me. We had to turn in our
gas masks, which made sense. I got to keep the inserts—pre-
scription glasses—OK. I might need them sometime and no
one else could use them, anyway. (If you know someone who
needs a pair of gas mask inserts, let me know. I have a pair I
haven't used in over thirty years.) I was going home. Our
Freedom Bird was supposed to be World Airways.
Remember World Airways? What anticipation!—American
stewardesses (no stewards in those days, just stewardesses),
great food (even airline food is great after a year of C rats),
soft cushy seats and clean airline bathrooms (no more cat
holes—know what I mean?). About six hours before board-
ing time the PA loudspeakers blared out an unwelcome
announcement. A *very* unwelcome announcement. Our
flight was being delayed for three (as in 3) days. Three whole,
long days. Why, guys were known to get killed in mortar
attacks at LBJ with only a one-day delay. Not a morale

builder, as you can understand. Well, about the time every-body was sitting around feeling sorry for themselves or get-ting plastered on American beer (none of that "33"), another announcement came over the PA. This one was welcome, indeed. At least as far as I was concerned. Seems as how there was a C141 Air Force cargo plane going to take off in a cou-ple of hours. All of us booked on the World Airways civilian airliner could wait the three days for it or we could get on the C141 right now and be on our way. Guess what! You're right. We did exactly what you would have done. We all piled onto that cargo plane quicker than ASAP. No matter that the seats were facing the back hatch where our baggage was piled. No matter that the "stewardess" was an ugly, crusty old tech ser-geant. No matter that the clean, nice bathroom was a latrine at the front by the cockpit (clean, but no luxury—so what). No matter that the airline food was a brown-bag Air Force sandwich "served" (tossed out) by that ugly sergeant. No matter at all. We were going home and that C141 was our welcome Freedom Bird!

I don't know your Freedom Bird story, but I'm sure it's not that much different from mine. Remember? I guess you'd have flown out on a Piper Cub for a Freedom Bird if that would have gotten you out of the 'Nam and back home. Arriving home and all the stuff involved with that is a differ-ent story. We all have our stories and they're all different. Some happy, some not. Some welcome home, some nothing. Some to family and friends, a few to just the dog, maybe. But for the Freedom Bird, I think we all were happy and full of joy just to see the silver wings or the red tail of the civilian air-liner, or even the olive drab of the C141 or C130. No matter. A Freedom Bird was a Freedom Bird. Freedom was *freedom*.

This all makes me think of a part of the Bible that I hope you'll let me share. Naturally, being a free person you can stop reading now. But I'd still like to share some words of Jesus that are just as important for our freedom as the Freedom Birds of Viet Nam. Jesus had responded to some people who had believed in him. This is what he had to say about freedom: "Jesus said to the people who believed in him, 'You are truly my disciples if you keep obeying my teachings. And you will know the truth, and the truth will set you free.' 'But we are descendants of Abraham,' they said. 'We have never been slaves to anyone on earth. What do you mean, 'set free?' Jesus replied, 'I assure you that everyone who sins is a slave of sin. A slave is not a permanent member of the family, but a son is part of the family forever. So if the Son sets you free, you will indeed be free.'" This is from the Bible New Testament book of John, chapter 8 and verses 32 through 36 (NLT). It's not hard to see that we are stuck in what God calls sin. It's not hard to see what Jesus was talking about and that it fits us only too well. What Jesus was talking about was that we also can be part of the family of God and be free of our sin through faith and belief in him. Same as those he was talking to, which I just quoted. Think about it. It would be fine if you'd get out your Bible, or go buy one at Waldenbooks or somewhere, and check it out for yourself.

Well, I'll finish this off for now. There's a lot to share about Freedom Birds from Viet Nam as you know plenty well, firsthand. There's a lot more to share about the freedom of your heart and soul that you may or may not know first-hand. That's between you and God, between you and Jesus. What I know, firsthand, is that my time in Viet Nam changed my life in ways that will last 'til the day I die. I'm a stronger man because of it, but that doesn't mean it was all bench presses and jogging. Strength from the Viet Nam experience came through the fire and testing. What I also know first-hand as well as from the Word of God, which I take as authoritative, is that freedom from the curse of sin has changed my life even more. Maybe you know what I mean. Maybe you don't. But you can know. Read it. Check it out. It's great to be free. Nothing like it. That's what Freedom Birds were all about. In more ways than one. Got it?

38

freedom birds, the sequel

"WHAT GOES UP HAS TO COME DOWN." KNOW WHAT I mean? No? I'll explain. You throw a ball up into the air and it's going to come down. Right? That's natural. Bullets too. Shoot them up. They come down—somewhere. Same with airplanes. They go up and then they come back down. Agreed? Good thing too, because if they didn't you'd be a space alien from Earth.

Now here's the point. It's about the title of this chapter which is "Freedom Birds—the Sequel." Remember when we talked about Freedom Birds? It was in another chapter. The one before this, I think. Maybe you didn't read it. Maybe you forgot. Maybe you tried to forget but couldn't. OK. Anyway, that chapter was about Freedom Birds and how great they were, a Freedom Bird being the airplane that took you to freedom. It meant getting out of Viet Nam permanently. It meant going back to the land of the Big PX. It meant being clean and safe and comfortable and riding around in cars instead of tracks (tanks, ACavs or any tracked vehicle). Mostly, it just meant going home to the good ole US of A. That was freedom and the Freedom Bird was how you'd get there.

When that bird went up, it was going to come back down on home soil. That's the sequel. Every one of us has a story about how we came home. Some got a Welcome Home! Some didn't, sad to say. Homecomings were sometimes wonderful and sometimes not. For this story I'm talking about the good part of coming home that we all experienced. We're not forgetting our buddies who didn't come home. We're not forgetting those who came home to the VA Hospital. We're not forgetting other stuff that you and I will *never* forget. Concerning Freedom Birds, we talked before about how spectacular it was to see the tail of that Continental Airways, that TWA, that Pan Am airliner or that C141 as it cruised our way—how we got on board and how we went sort of berserk when we got out of Viet Nam airspace and headed home.

The sequel to all this about Freedom Birds taking off from the Nam was that they also came down where we wanted to be. That's what I'm talking about—taking off from Viet Nam being the story and landing at home the sequel. I won't ever forget the feeling. I don't even want to forget that feeling of landing at Travis Air Force Base on U.S. soil. We disembarked (meaning we got off the airplane), went through the terminal and got on a civilian highway cruiser out at the curb. It was so cool in that wonderful bus. It rode so smooth. How luxurious it was to be inside a clean bus out there on that paved freeway in the Land of the Big PX—*home*! I looked across the American countryside and it was so beautiful! I kid you not, all the way from Travis to the San Francisco airport, I saw not one single bomb crater. I saw not one single hole in the road blown by a land mine. I saw absolutely no soldiers guarding the bridges. I saw not one single red Honda 50 with three riders or smoky Lambretta with fifteen passengers. I saw not one person in black pajamas who could have been a rice farmer by day and a VC by night. I saw not one ARVN check point. Why, and you don't have to believe this, you would hardly have known from that wonderful bus ride that we were even in a war! Isn't that remarkable?

But on to even more remarkable things: We got to the airport. Wow! Speaking of luxury! There were all these

Americans running around and not one of them had a weapon—no M16s, no 45s, no steel pots, no grenades, no canteens either. Can you believe it? And speaking of wonderful—that airport looked as beautiful as a king's palace to me. And not a single bullet hole to be seen. I'm here to tell you, those first impressions when I came home to America were powerful and profound and you know what I mean. How long has it been since you thought about that?

I was truly overwhelmed to be home again. But I came home different from what I was when I left for the Nam. I had a new perspective on life and on being an American that I don't want to lose. For starts, I was reminded that we have it real nice in this country. That's easy to forget. Coming home from a year in Viet Nam made me realize how much better we have it here than most of the world.

These past few years, many have come to realize, more than before, just how blessed we are to be Americans. How blessed we are to be a part of the USA. How honored we are as vets that we made our contribution to the greatness of this land. Most Americans recognize the contribution of the Viet Nam vet even if a few don't. But I want *you* to recognize it. The fall of the Berlin Wall, Desert Storm, the liberation of Iraq, the surge of patriotism following 9/11, building memorials for WWII and Korean War vets and other good things have happened largely because of what we did in Viet Nam. I'm not blowing smoke. I mean these things and see that they are true. I hope you see it too.

So do you catch what I mean by "Freedom Birds—the Sequel"? Our story about Freedom Birds taking off from Viet Nam is the story. Landing back in the USA—that's the sequel to the story. Clear? Each part of the story means a lot, more than just a take-off from Viet Nam and a landing in America, which each of us lived. This country means far more for you and me than it would without the Viet Nam experience. We have a perspective on America's greatness that the protected will never know. You know what I mean.

There's another Freedom Bird coming for each of us too. It's a lot more important than a C141 or a TWA airliner. I haven't taken it yet. You haven't either, because it's the last ride. It's the end of the trail. Some call it crossing over Jordan. Some call it kicking the bucket. In Viet Nam we said his number was up. We can say he wrote the book. We can call it whatever we want. The fact is that that our last flight is coming. We all have our Freedom Bird from this life. It's up to each of us what our sequel will be—where we'll come down. I'll be coming down in the Kingdom of God, otherwise known as Heaven. This is the place Jesus described when he said, "I am going there to prepare a place for you. And if I go and prepare a place for you, I will come back and take you to be with me that you may be where I am" (John 14:2, 3).

Our Freedom Bird over three decades ago was an unforgettable event following a profound experience. When the Freedom Bird came and took off, it was time to leave. I knew where I was going—back home to the USA. It's where I started and where I knew I belonged. The sequel was when I landed. It was great to be home because it was the land I loved and where I wanted to be. When I take my last Freedom Bird, the one from this life, I know what that sequel will be too. I know where I'll come down. It will be in heaven where I'll belong and want to be. I hope the same for you.

39

a proud legacy

"IRAQI FREEDOM." HOW DOES THAT SOUND TO YOU? IT hasn't been so long since that war was fought with great "shock and awe." Today, as I write, our troops have completed their job of deposing Saddam Hussein and taking out his evil regime. From what I've seen, it made the Iraqi people very happy. And that's an understatement. Did you follow the war? I did. Just as I followed Desert Storm a decade before. Back then I was still on active duty at Fort Huachuca, Arizona. There have also been other conflicts in the years since we served in Viet Nam. But these two wars against the brutal terrorist regime in Iraq have been particularly significant for us as Viet Nam vets. At least, that's my opinion after going to Viet Nam for two tours and still being on active duty for Desert Storm.

I remember when our troops came home from Desert Storm, how they were given parades and joyous celebrations of welcome. The whole country was in a party mood for them. I remember that many Viet Nam vets were bitter about how well these troops were welcomed home. This was in contrast to how we were shipped home like so much freight, dumped onto the air base tarmac and left to fend for ourselves in a frequently hostile America. Not only were there no welcomes or parades, but there was a whole lot of nasty *un*welcoming activity making clear for too many that the warrior was seen as an object of disgust rather than as the hero that he really was. The silent majority didn't see it that way. But they were silent.

Now, let's acknowledge that this is all true, at least as a broad generalization. *However,* let's *also* acknowledge that a whole lot of water has flowed under the bridge since our "homecoming." This was true at Desert Storm time and it's true now. With the building of The Wall in Washington, DC and the realization by Americans that the news media, Hollywood, and a lot of politicians were spinning reality, perceptions changed 100 percent toward the warrior, separating him from perceptions about the war. These days, Viet Nam vets are held in very high regard by almost all Americans. I say this even though schools are not teaching the subject adequately and people are confused about the real history of that major event. It's gotten to the point where there are Viet Nam vet wannabes all over the place that want a piece of the action. How's that for a change of national attitude?

Come back with me in your memories to those parades we gave our Desert Storm troops. In the lessons-learned department, have you ever stopped to realize that the reason those parades were so hearty and joyous was largely because Americans felt guilty for how they brought their Viet Nam vets home? And they should have felt guilty, because they were. But have you ever stopped to think that those young Desert Storm troops were your own kids? Would you deny this recognition to your own kids? I don't think so. Be happy that they got what you didn't. Be happy that they got what you paid for. It's a part of your legacy. Be proud. I think you'll agree that our Desert Storm vets would have had their parades and welcome home parties anyway. However, their welcomes would not have been nearly as extravagant if not for the dues paid by their Viet Nam vet forbears, their dads and uncles, who, themselves, were brought home in such a shameful way.

Here we are years later. Now we welcome a new generation of warriors home from war. Back again from the sands
of Iraq and the Middle East. Or even Afghanistan or Kosovo.
It looks to me that we have a lot to celebrate again. It looks
to me like we're returning our own kids again from another
war. Except now many are our grandkids. So be happy. Viet
Nam vets paid a high price so these young men and women
could return home as heroes. This nation has learned to separate the soldier from the war. Even those who opposed taking out the brutal Saddam Hussein regime admit they must
support the warrior. That admission didn't come from any
genetic sense of goodness. It came because the nation
learned from the Viet Nam vet that you treat your warriors
with respect no matter what you think of those who sent
them to fight the wars. It's more of our proud legacy.

Other lessons learned from the Viet Nam warrior bene-
fit the young generation of our military in their service of
America. Look at the embedded reporters who were in Iraqi
Freedom. Some were in harm's way right along with the
troops. Even though it was only a few who put their money
where their mouth was, at least those were out there on the
edge. Others, including editors and publishers, stayed in
their ivory towers putting their usual spin on events. But lessons have been learned anyway. Those lessons came directly
from our experience with the media and political spinners
and agitators from the Viet Nam war.

There's an even more important event of a greater price
paid for a greater good. We understand paying a large price
for a greater good. We were part of such a price and we're
experiencing the greater good, such as freedom and speaking
English instead of Russian or whatever. We understand the
concept pretty well. The greater price I'm talking about was
that paid by God for the redemption of our very souls and
the fulfillment of the purpose for which we were born. A
verse in the Bible makes this clear. It's a popular verse. It takes
a lot of abuse and ridicule, which is strange, considering that

it's true and has the power to transform the life of anyone who accepts it. (We understand that sort of thing, don't we?) The verse is John 3:16-17: "For God so loved the world that he gave his one and only Son, that whoever believes in him shall not perish but have eternal life. For God did not send his son into the world to condemn the world, but to save the world through him."

It's clear that America has learned the lessons from Viet Nam that we must appreciate, respect, and celebrate the warriors who go to fight our nation's battles. I'm glad this has been learned. It's a proud legacy Viet Nam vets have given America. Our young troopers now come home from war to parades and appreciation from those who sent them. It's also clear that many appreciate what God has done for them through the price he paid for their salvation and purpose for living. That appreciation is given through accepting that offer of paid-up salvation and purpose through Jesus Christ, his Son. I've accepted that offer. Have you?

glossary

AO—Area of Operations, the geographical area assigned to each military unit for which it had responsibility.

ACav—Armored personnel carrier configured to carry extra weaponry and ammunition. It was used as a cavalry fighting and reconnaissance vehicle.

ACR—Armored Cavalry Regiment

Agent Orange—The chemical that was widely used throughout South Viet Nam to defoliate the heavy brush along the roads our troops travelled. This was for the purpose of clearing the vegetation so our troops could see in order to fight the enemy.

ARVN—Army of the Republic of Viet Nam. This was the army of South Viet Nam.

ASAP—As soon as possible.

AVLB—Armored Vehicle Launcher Bridge—This was a tank that carried a portable bridge on top which it could lay down for temporary situations.

Commo—Communication

dee-dee-mau—(Author's spelling). Soldiers slang in Viet Nam for "Get the ---- out of here fast."

DEROS—Date of estimated rotation from overseas service.

donut dollies—Young women employed by the military civilian Special Services to provide organized entertainment and refreshment for soldiers. Donuts were a common refreshment, hence the young women were affectionately called "donut dollies."

FSB—Fire support base.

MARS—The system of two-way radio and telephone connections that made it possible for soldiers in Viet Nam to talk to a loved one in the States.

MEDCAPS—Medical Civic Action Programs.

NVA—North Vietnamese Army

PCS—Permanent Change of Station

pro-jo—Projectiles, "bullets" fired by field artillery

PTSD—Post Trauma Stress Disorder. Traumatic experiences are a source of stress for anyone. It becomes a disorder when it's so exceptionally traumatic that the individual cannot cope with it. Often results from combat, rape, severe accidents, etc.

RPG—Rocket propelled grenade.

Sheridan—An armored track vehicle that was smaller than a tank and had a turret mounted main gun and machine guns similar to a tank.

sitrep—Situation report.

skunion—Very bad stuff, mostly being at the receiving end of lots of shooting and various other deadly happenings.

sling load—The cargo carried underneath a flying helicopter held by a strap, a sling, which was released in a designated area prior to landing.

TOC—Tactical Operations Center.

TRADOC—Training and Doctrines Command.

USAID—United States of America International Development.

VC—Viet Cong.

vill—Village.

Tales of Thunder Run
Order Form

Postal orders: Point Man Book Bunker
P.O. Box 627
Carson City, MI 48811

E-mail orders: pointmanben@cmsinter.net

Please send *Tales of Thunder Run* to:

Name: _____

Address: _____

City: _____ State: _____

Zip: _____

Telephone: (_____) _____

Book Price: $12.95

Shipping: $3.00 for the first book and $1.00 for each additional book to
cover shipping and handling within US, Canada, and Mexico.
International orders add $6.00 for the first book and $2.00 for
each additional book.

Or order from:
ACW Press
85334 Lorane Hwy
Eugene, OR 97405

(800) 931-BOOK

or contact your local bookstore